# Crayons
## coloring book

David Sorkin

ISBN 978-1-5308-9325-6

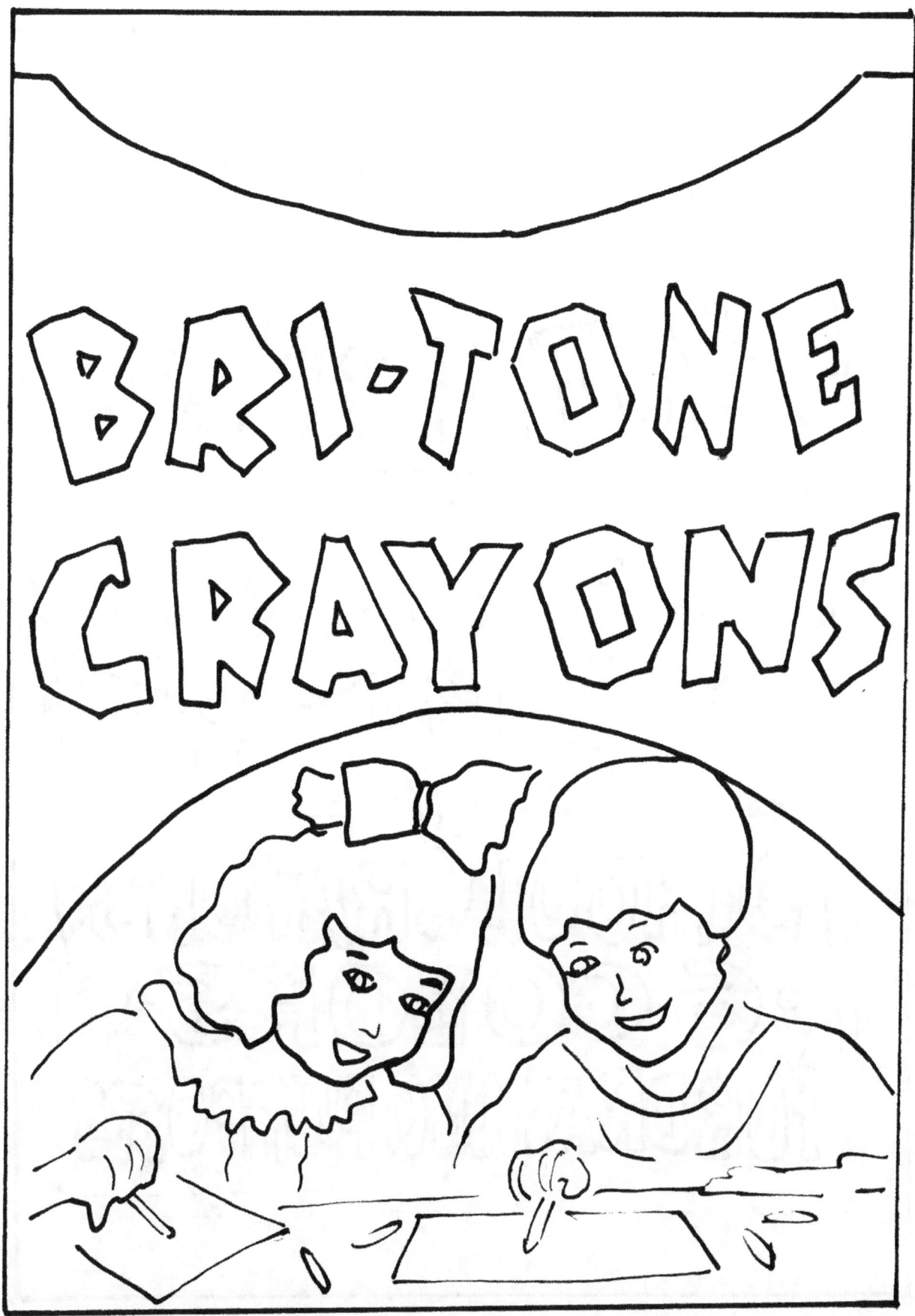

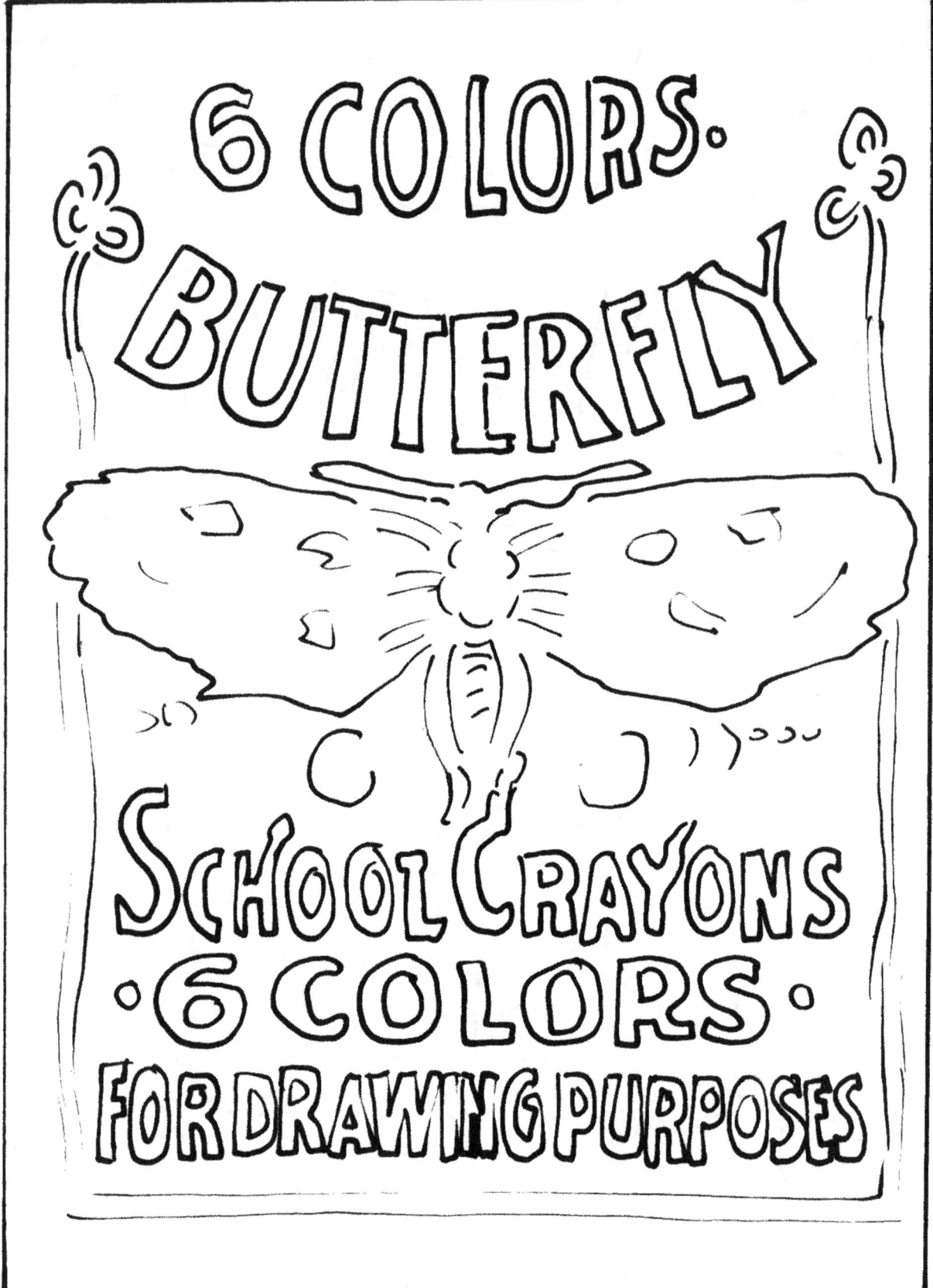

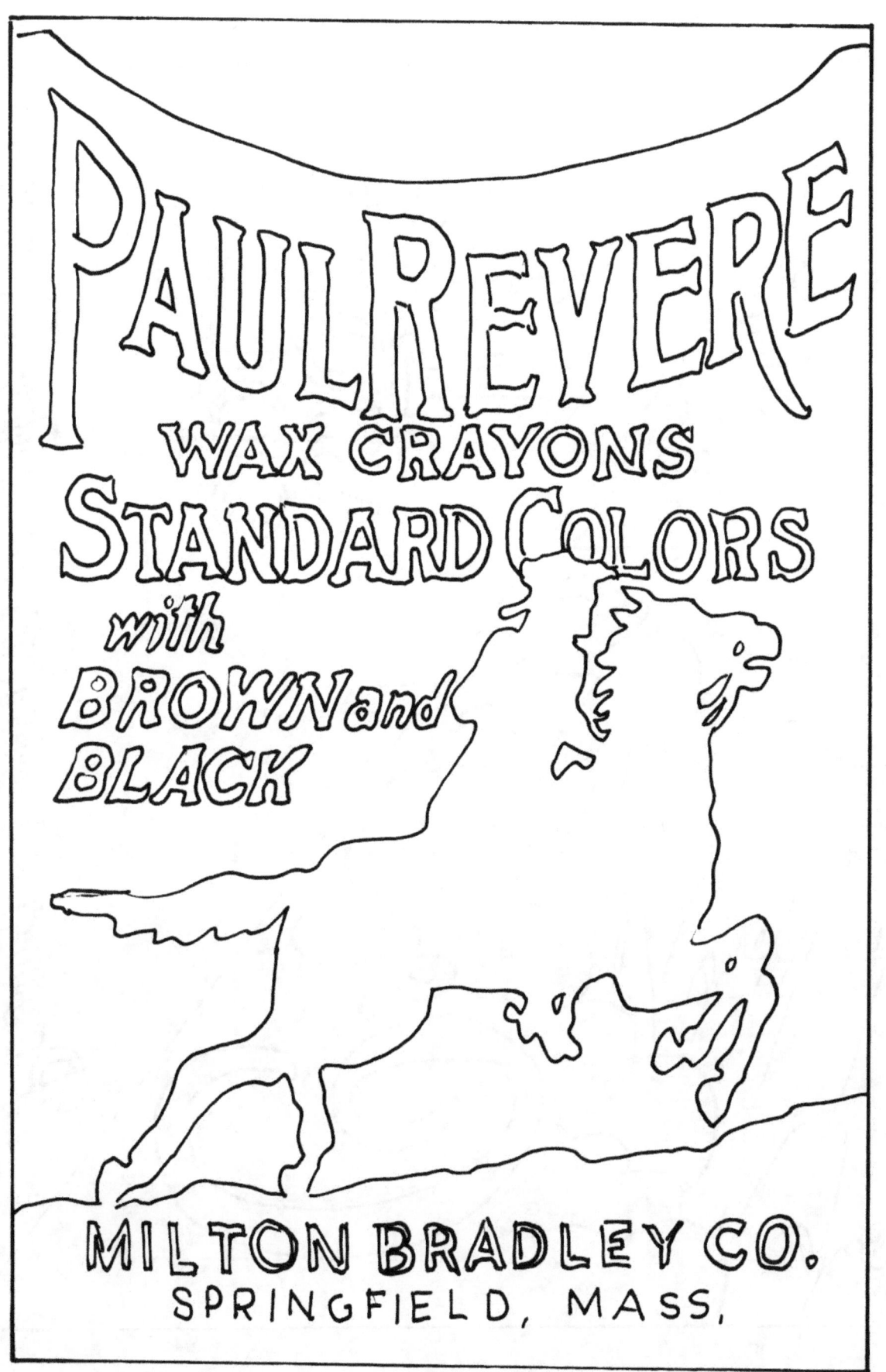

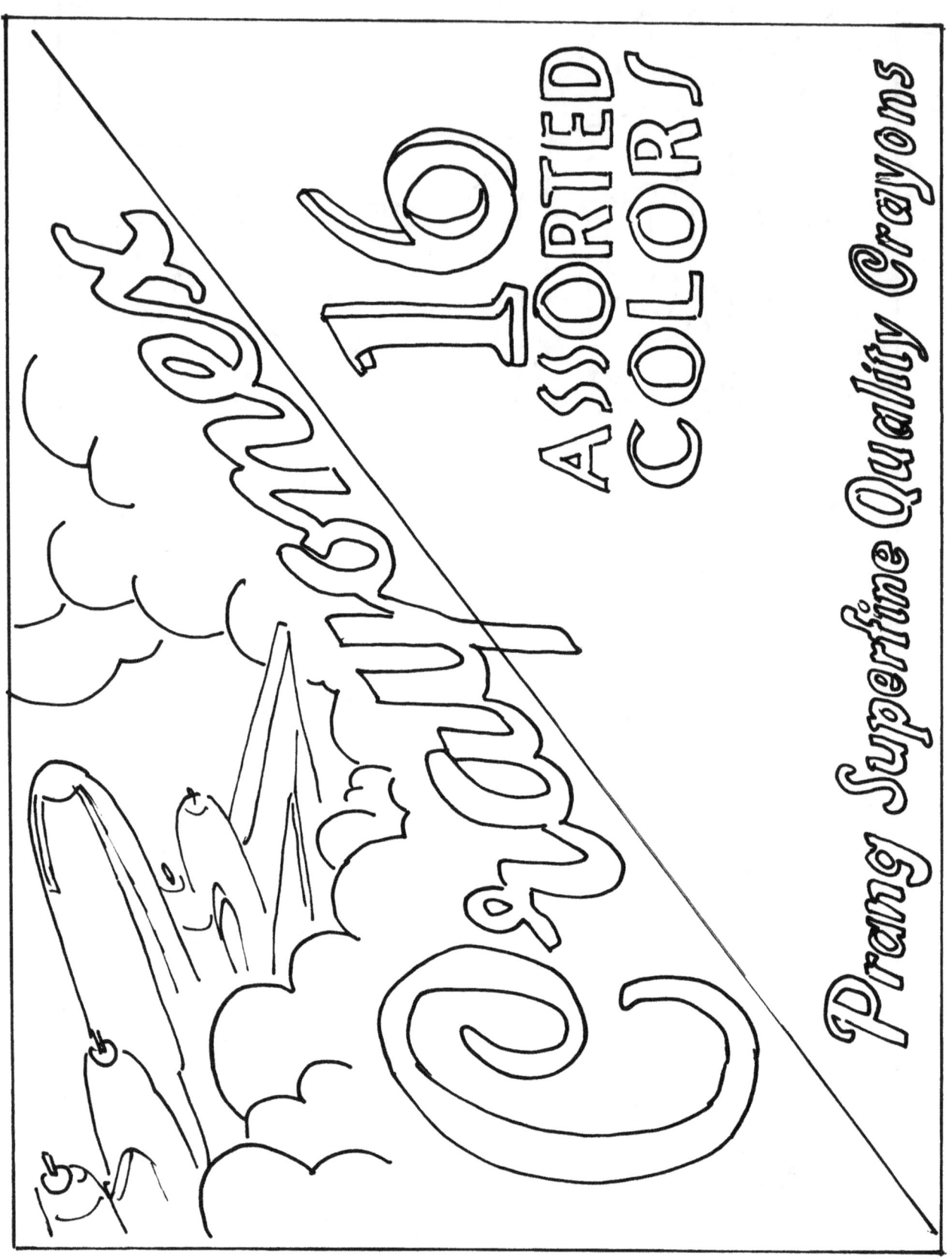

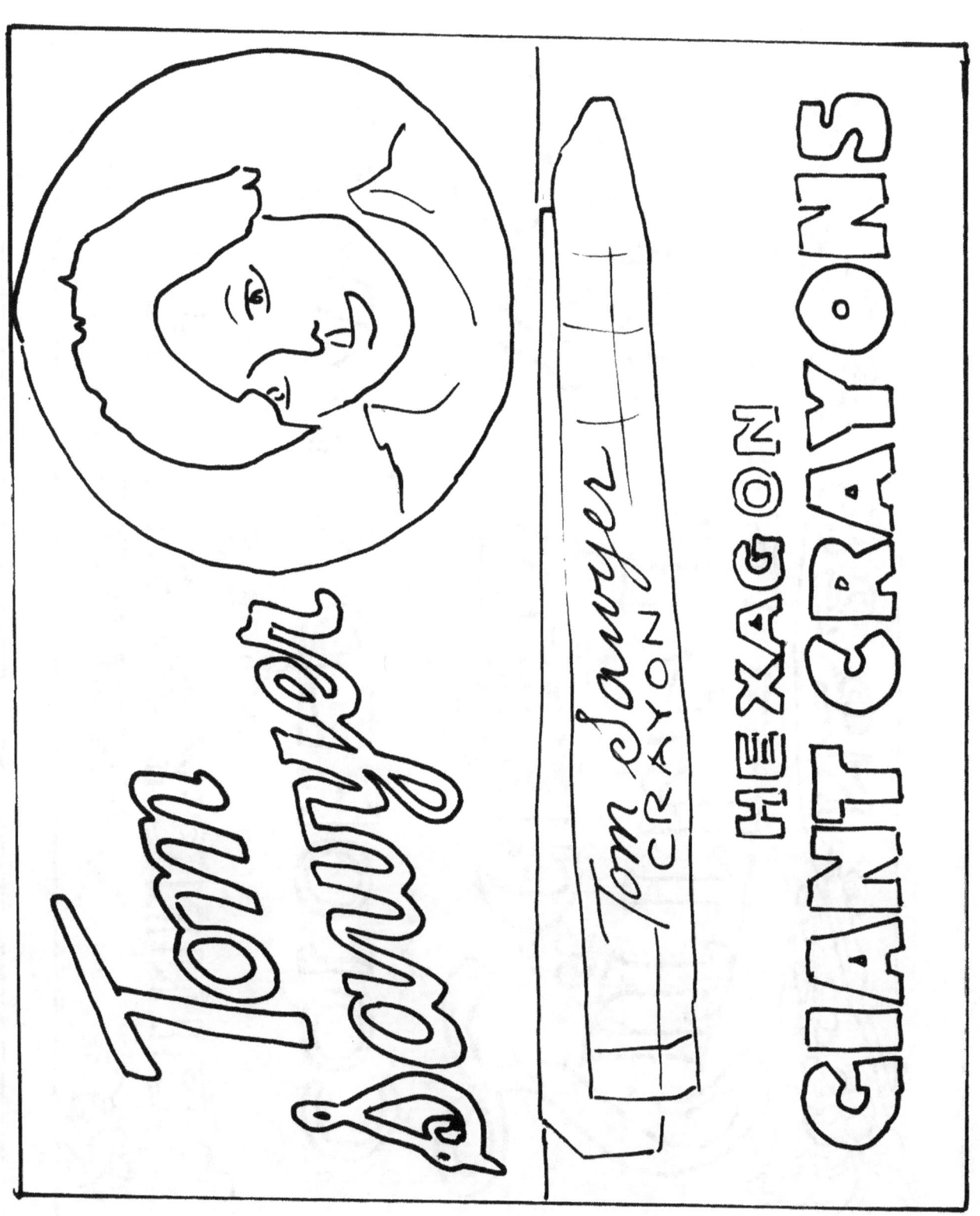

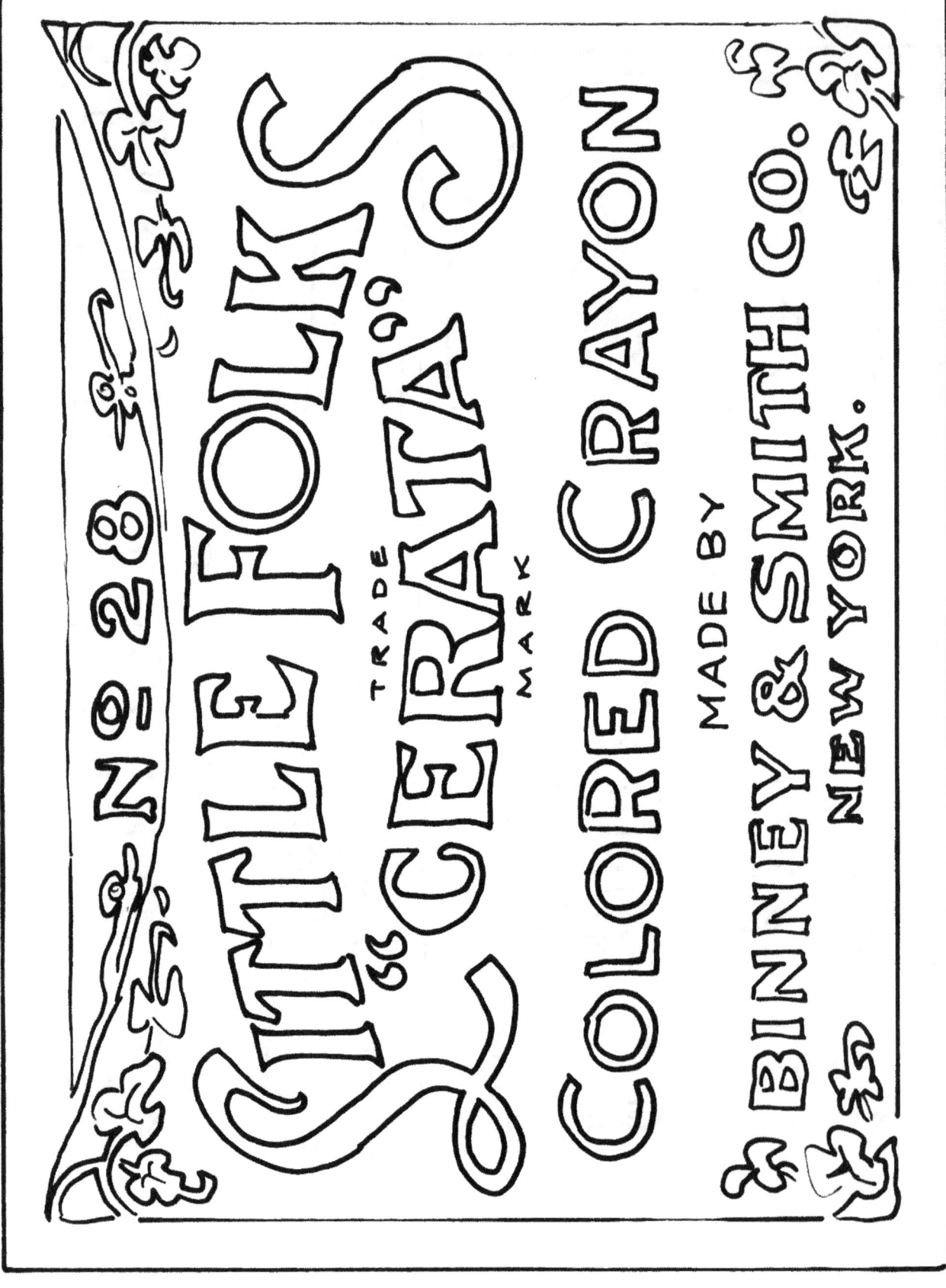

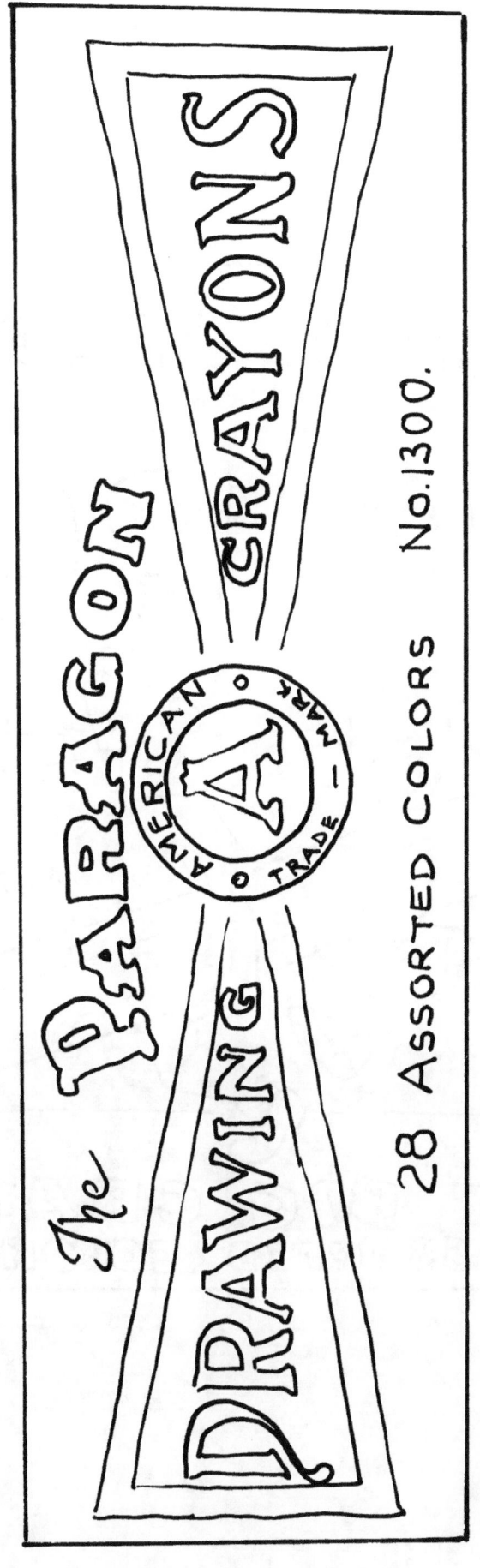

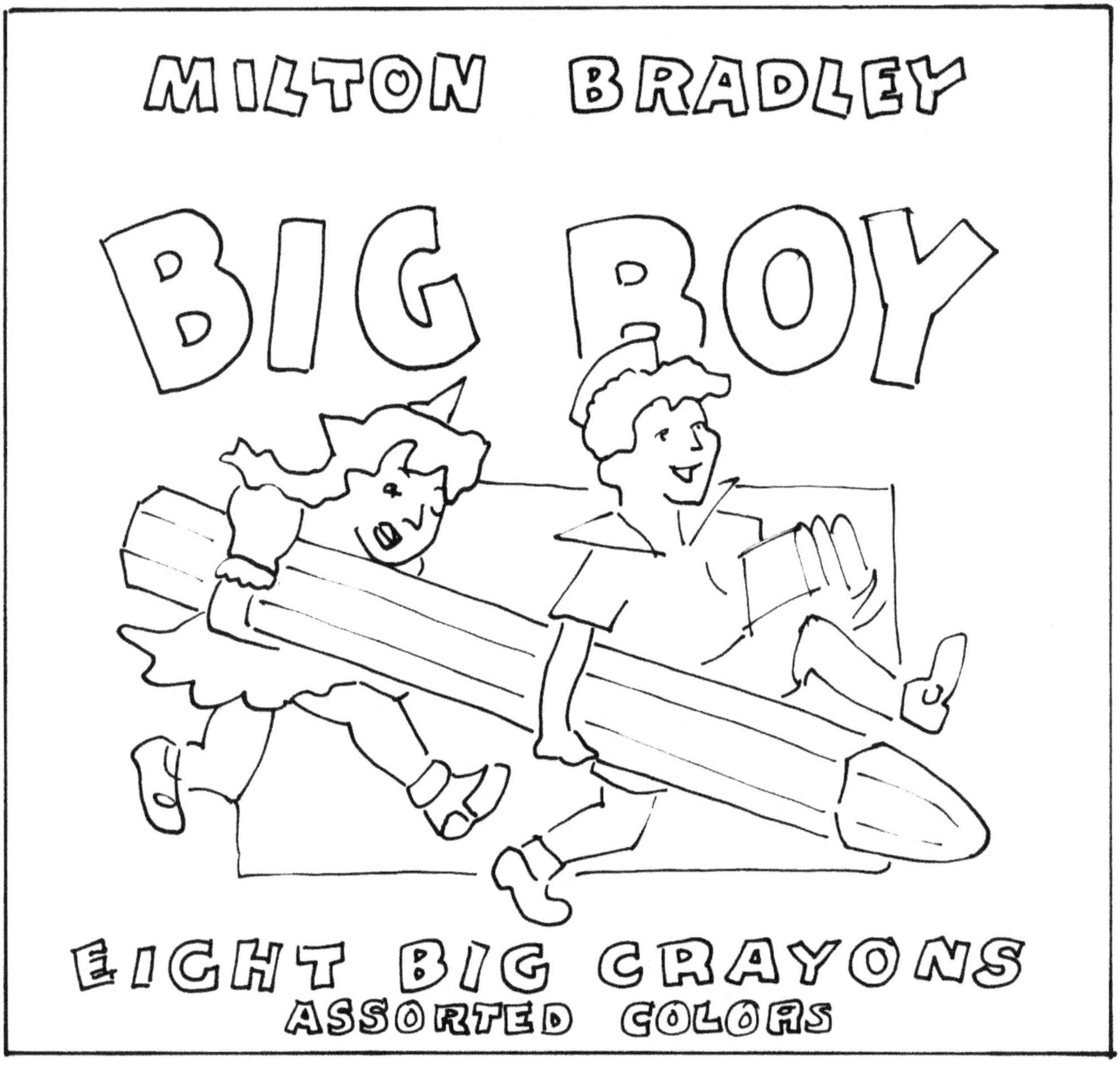
MILTON BRADLEY
BIG BOY
EIGHT BIG CRAYONS
ASSORTED COLORS

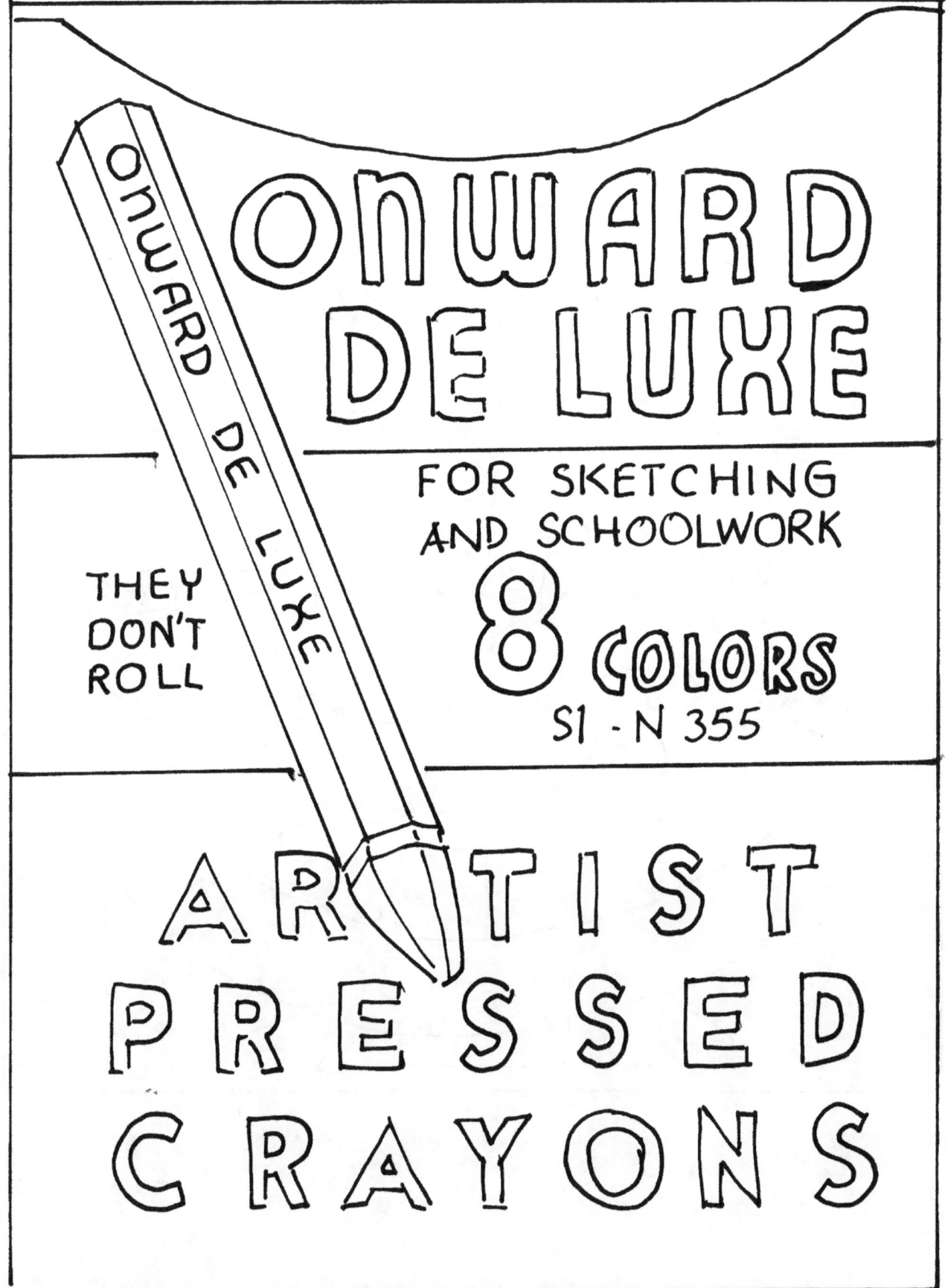

ONWARD DE LUXE

ONWARD DE LUXE

FOR SKETCHING
AND SCHOOLWORK

8 COLORS

S1 - N 355

THEY
DON'T
ROLL

ARTIST
PRESSED
CRAYONS

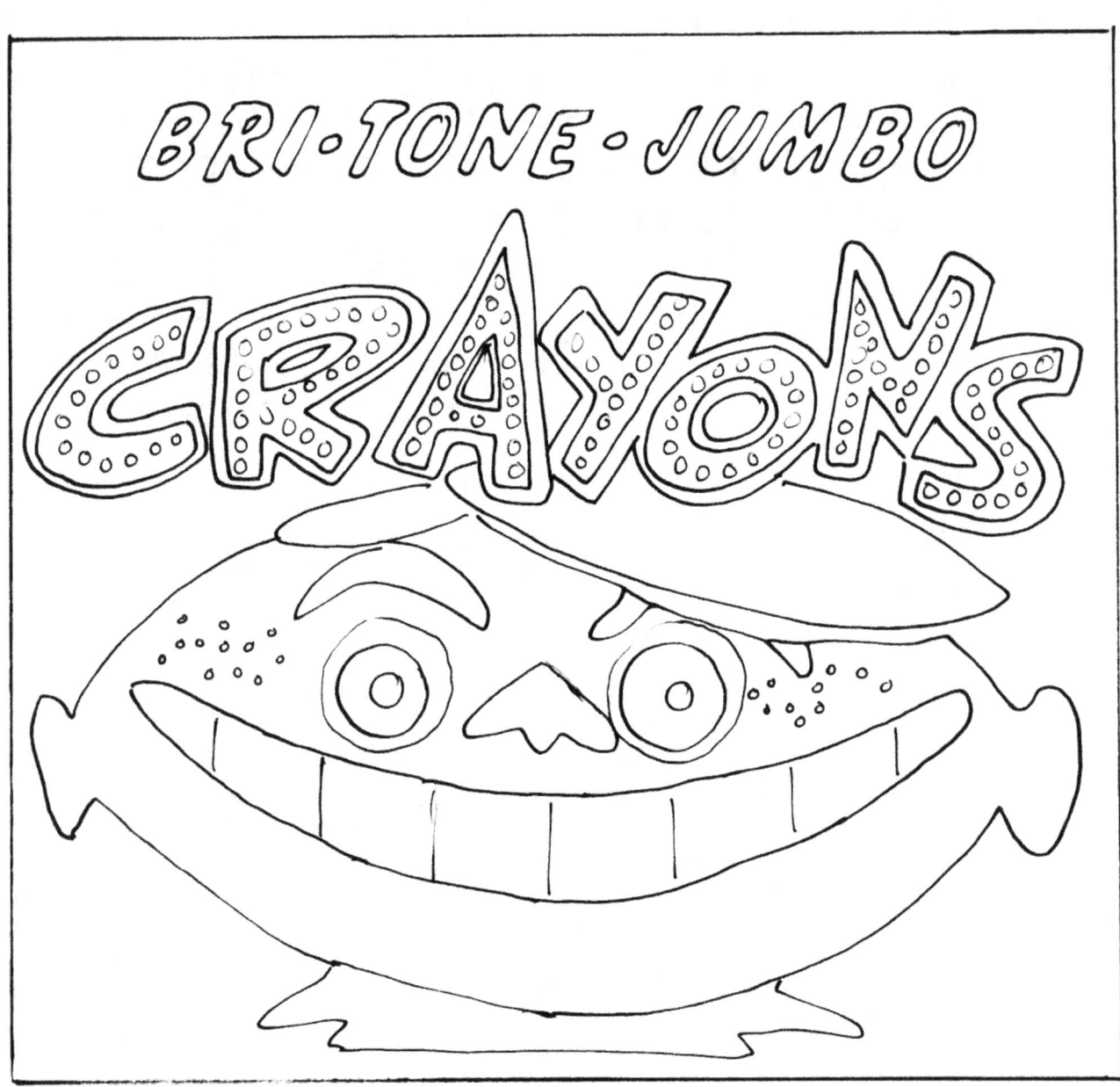

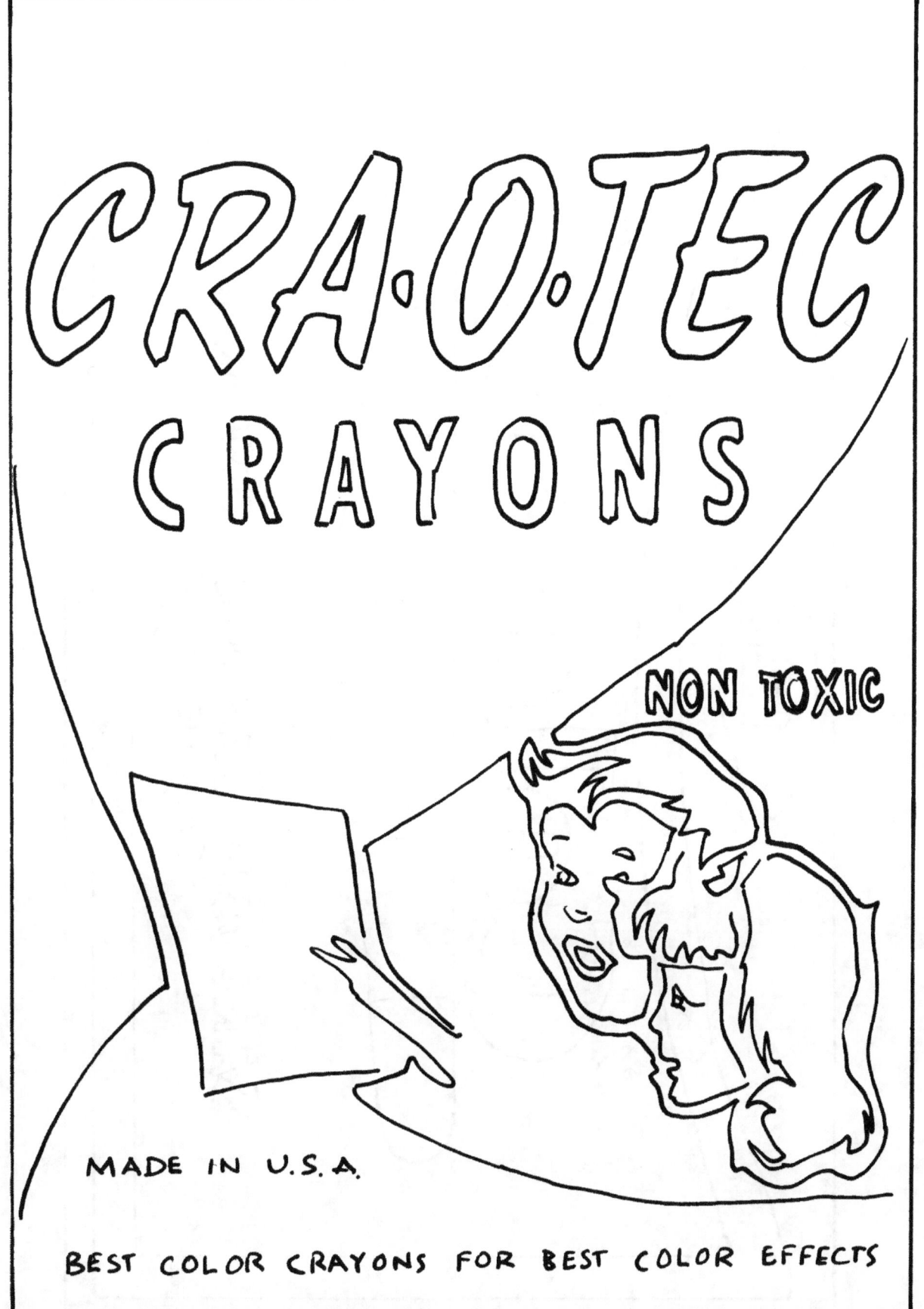

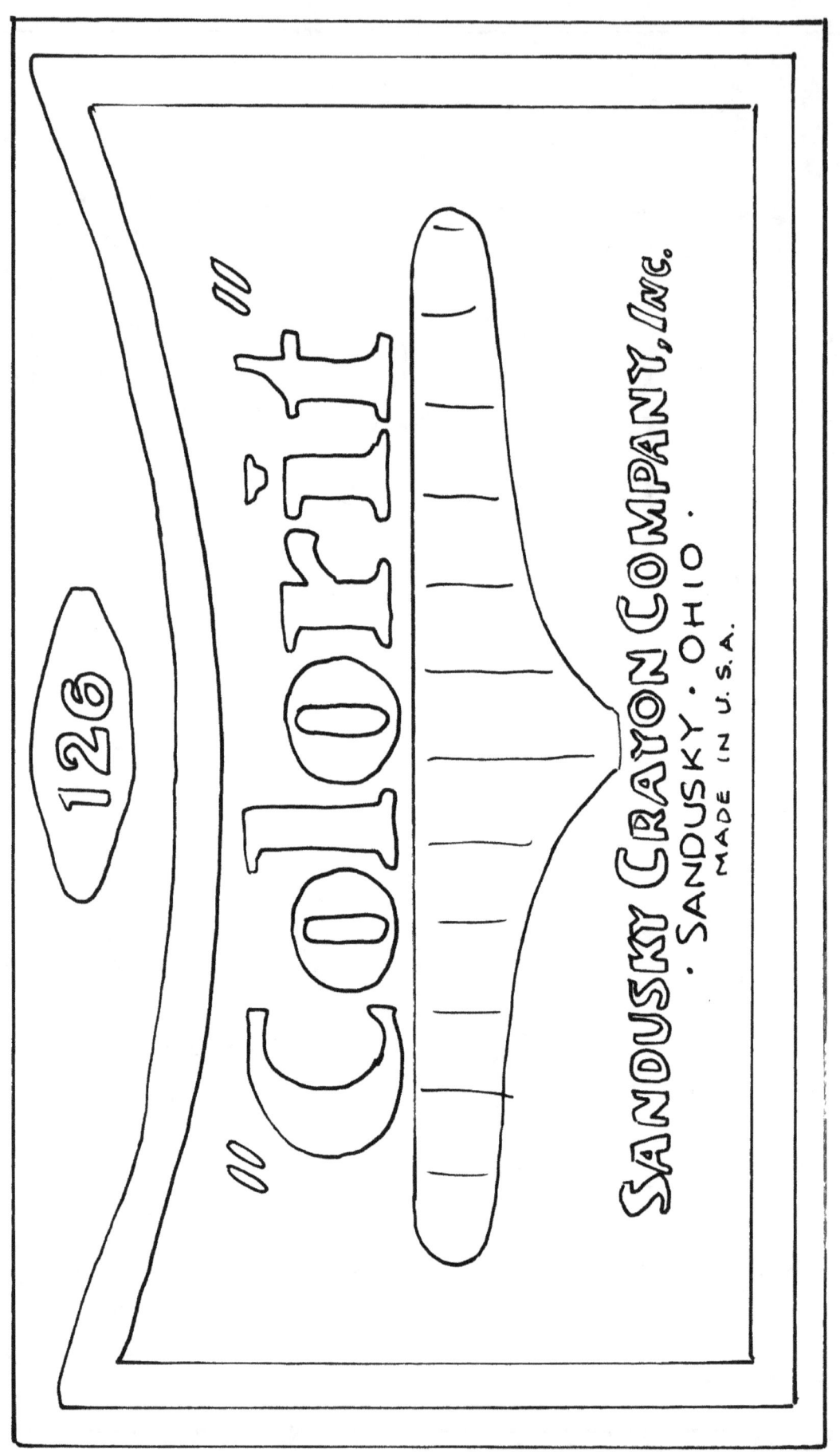

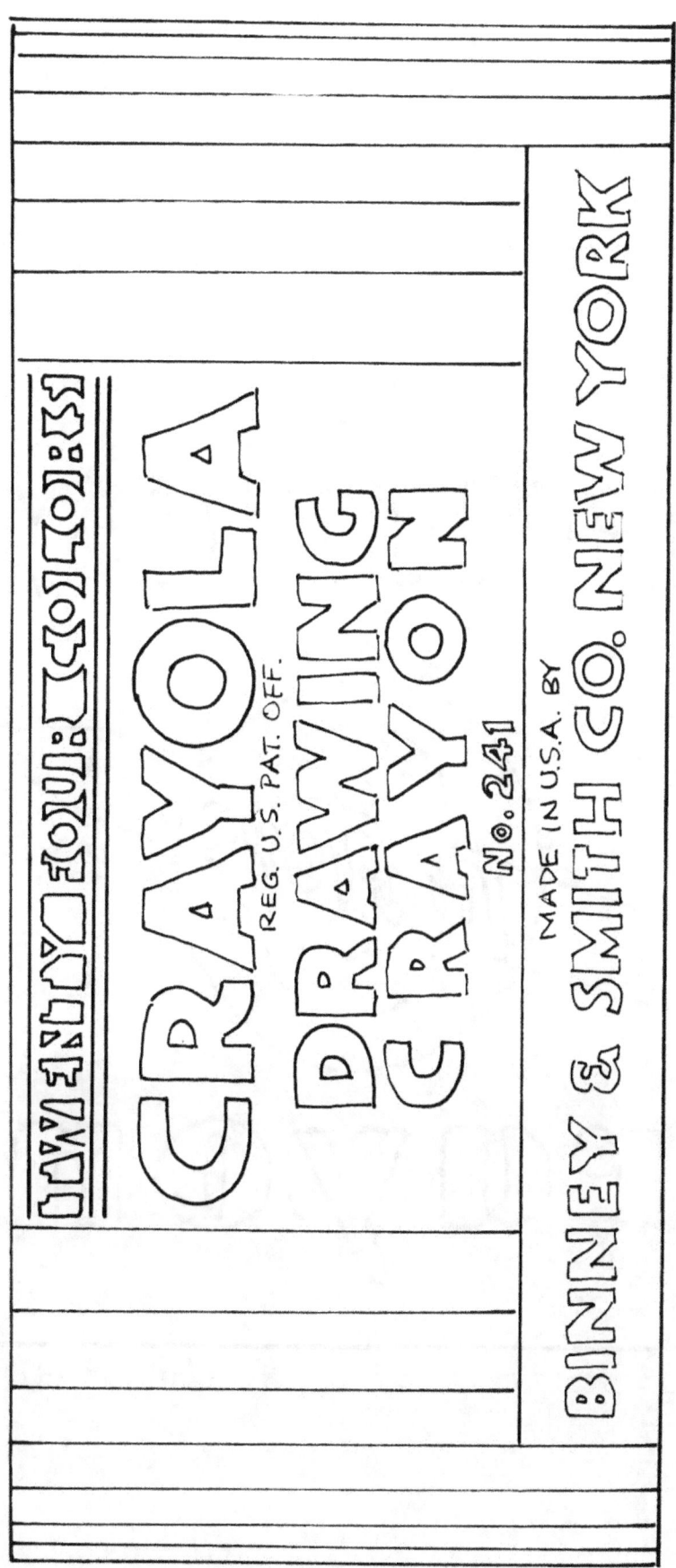

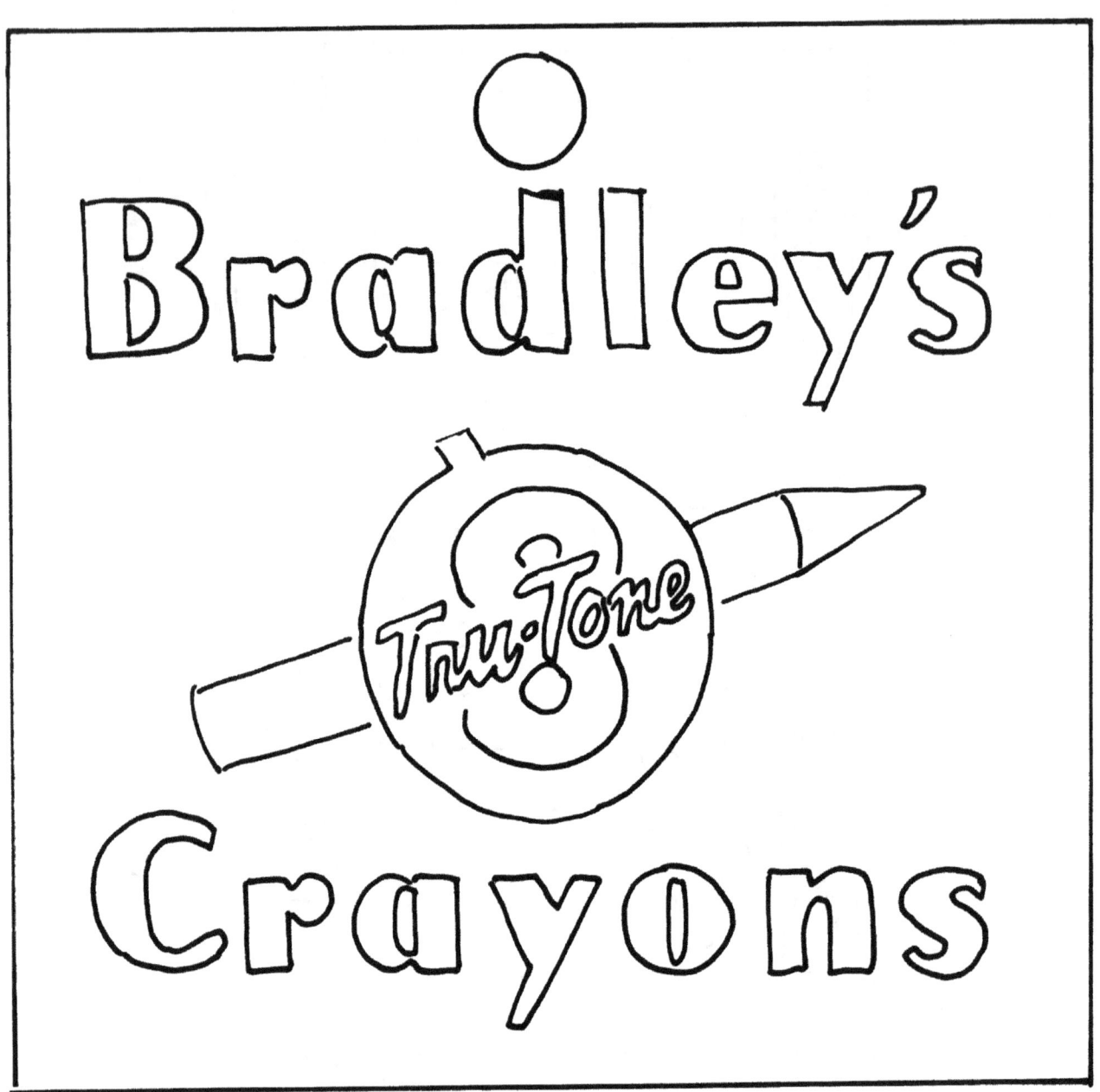

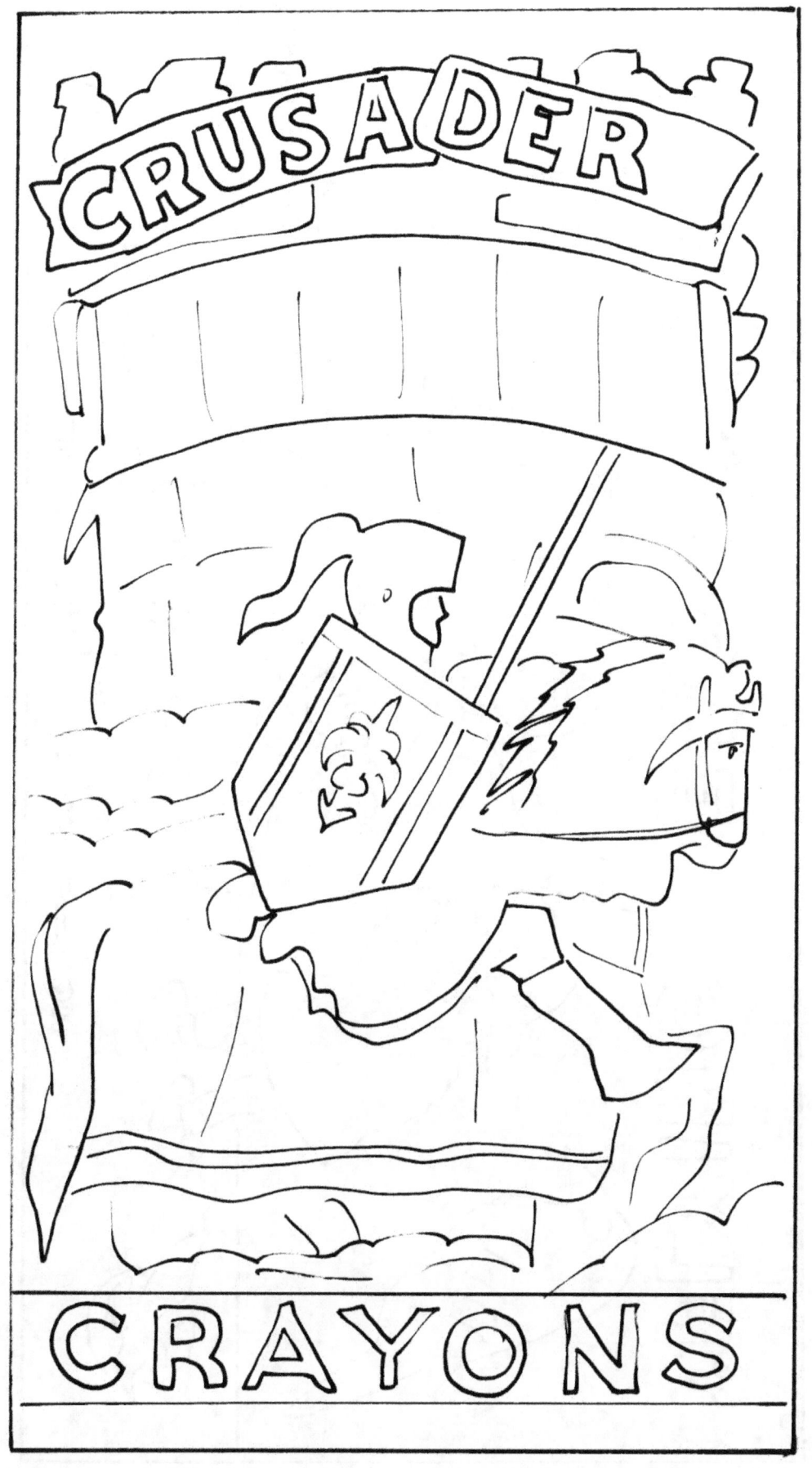

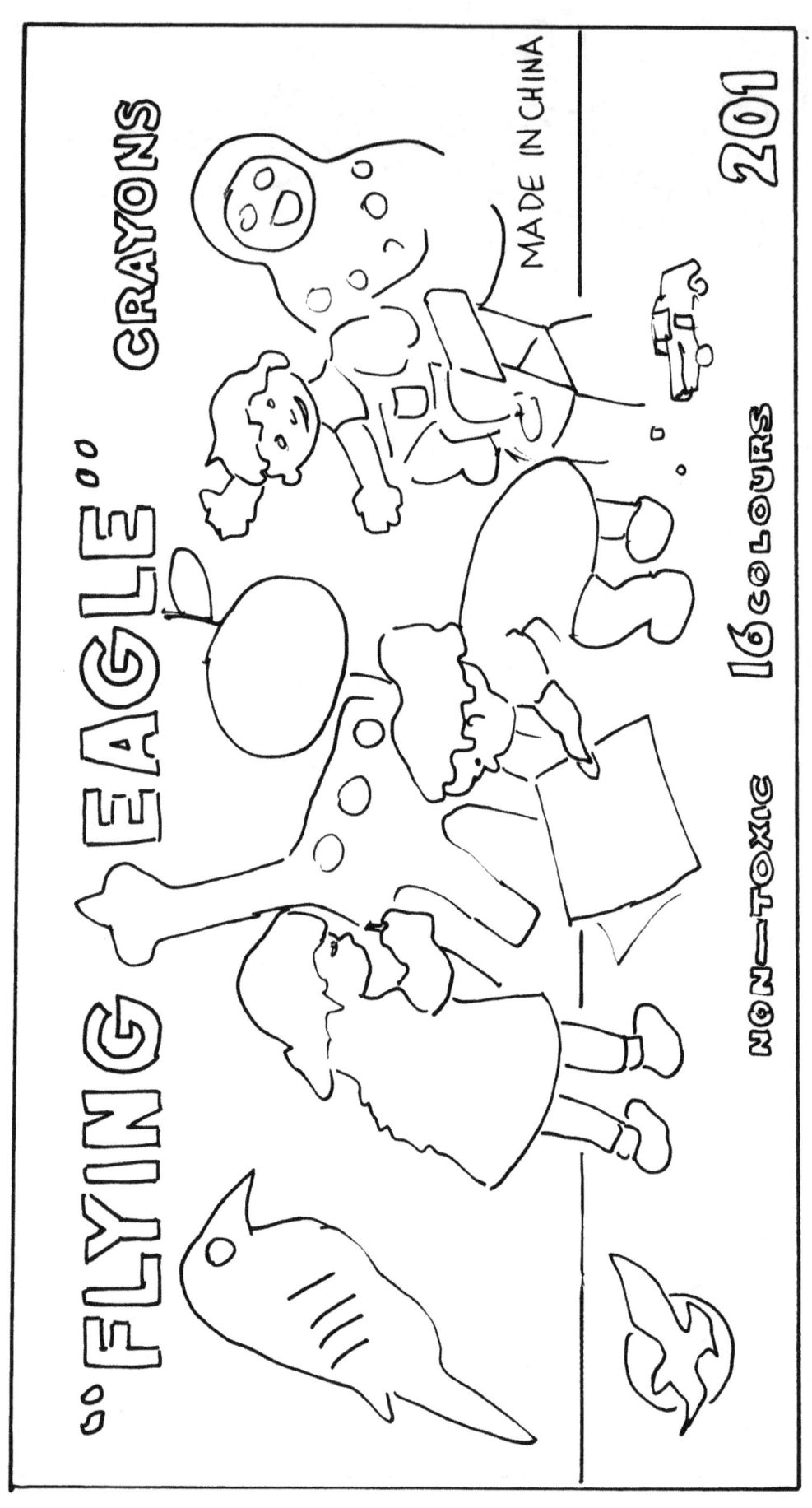

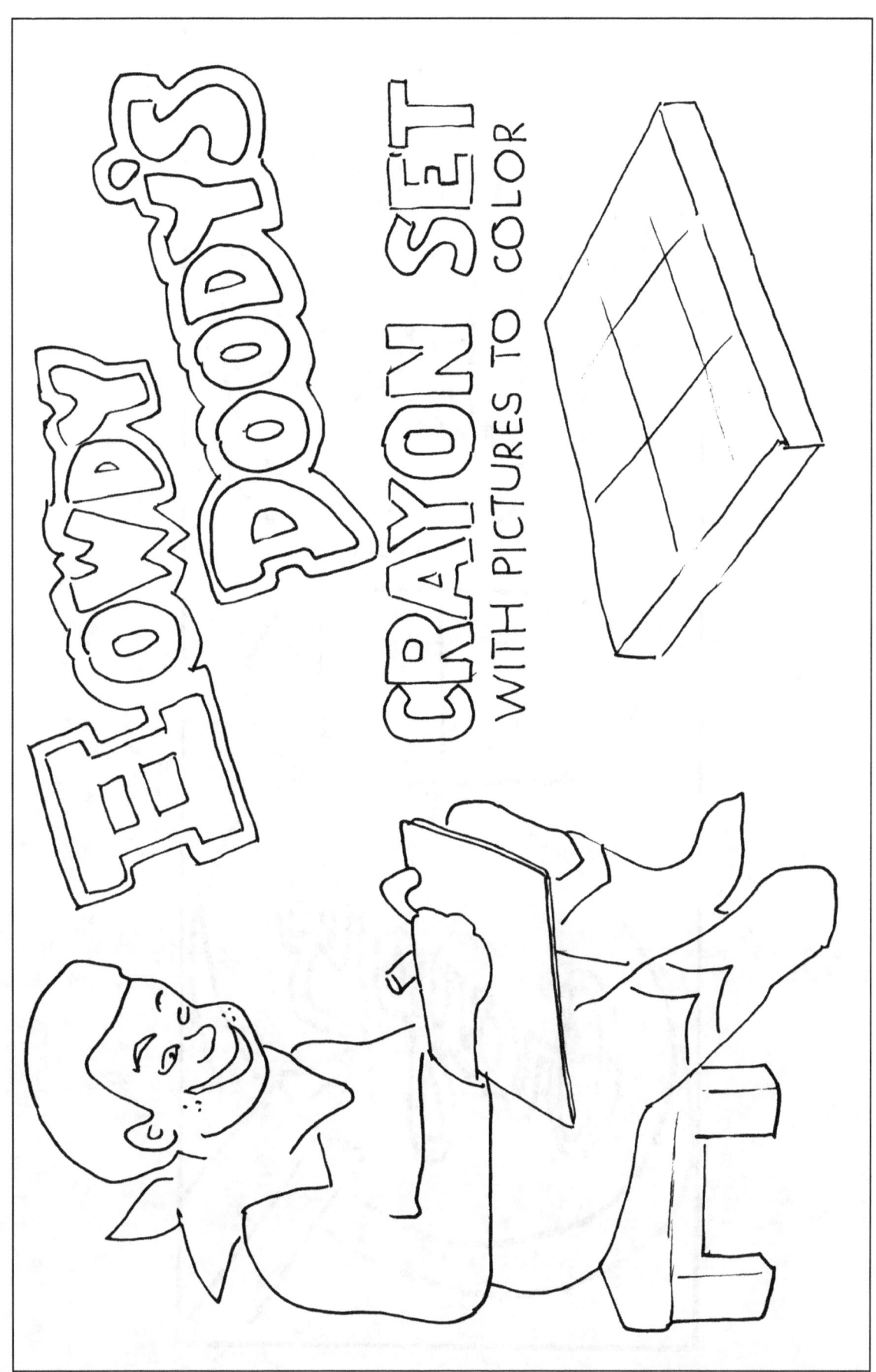

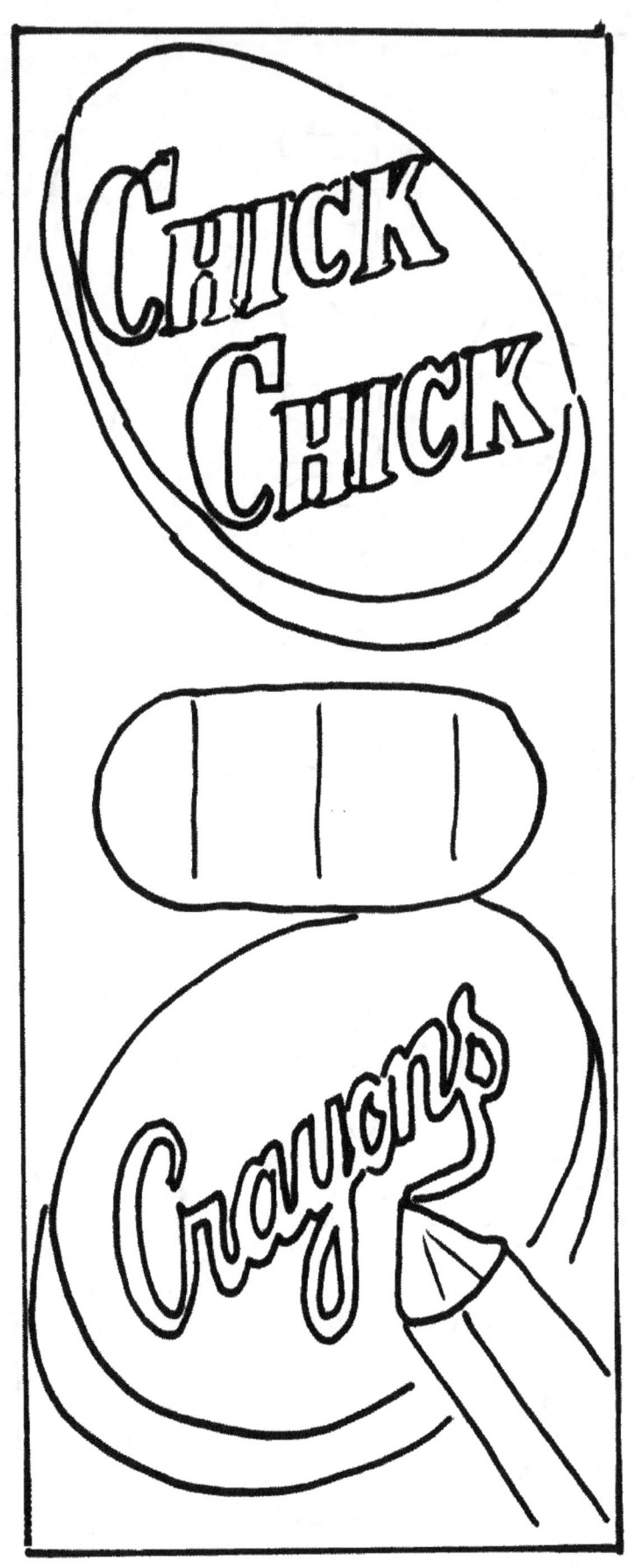

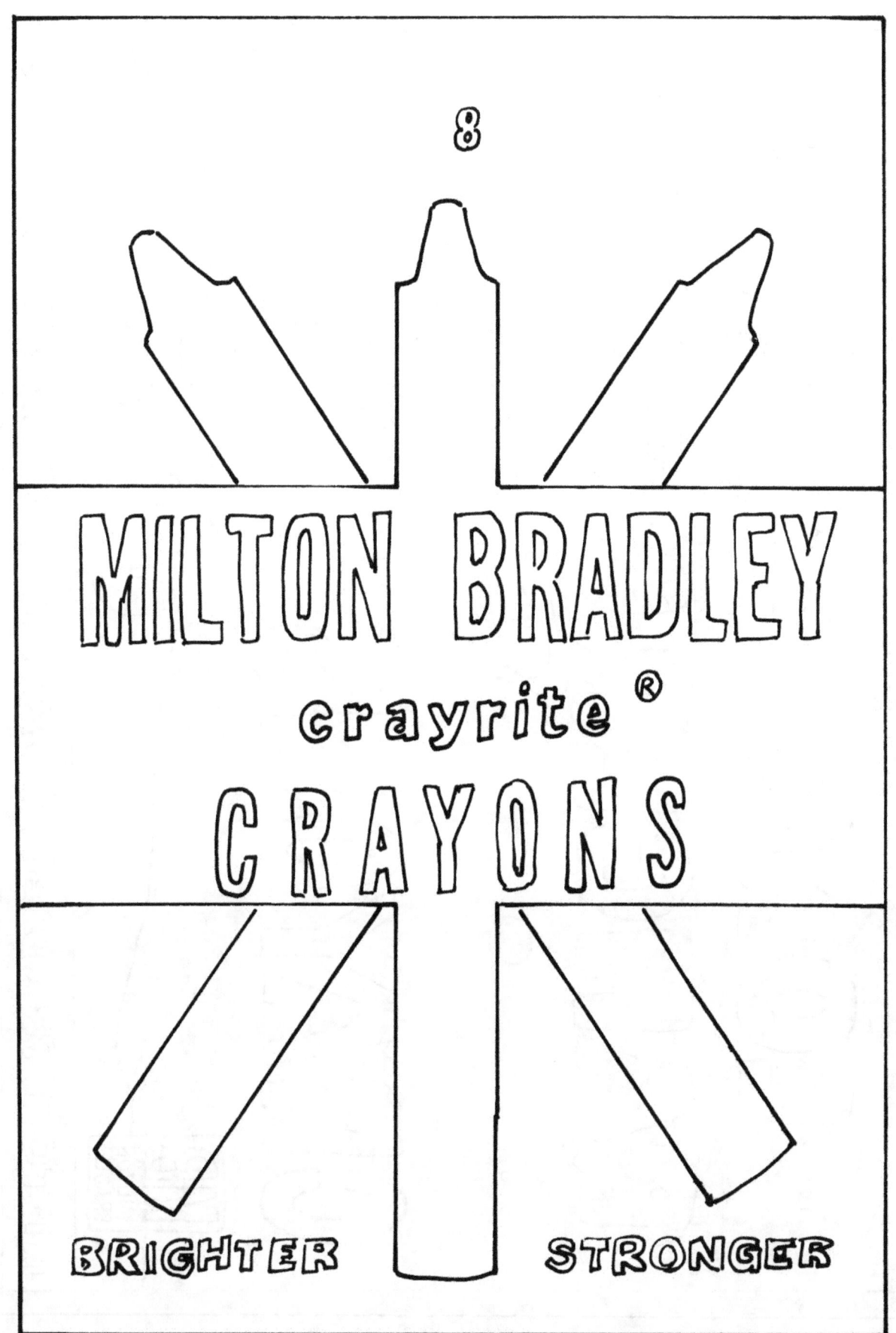

19

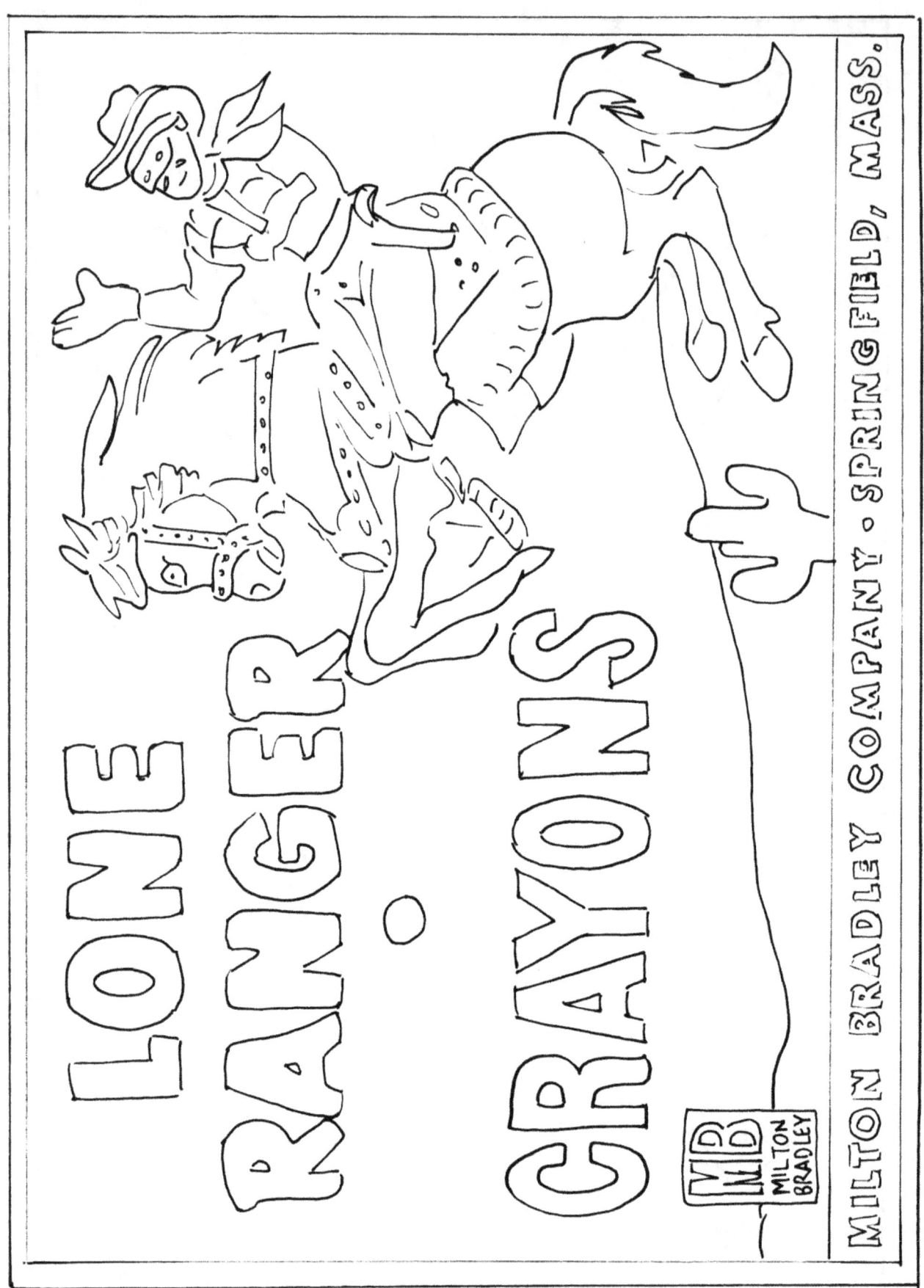

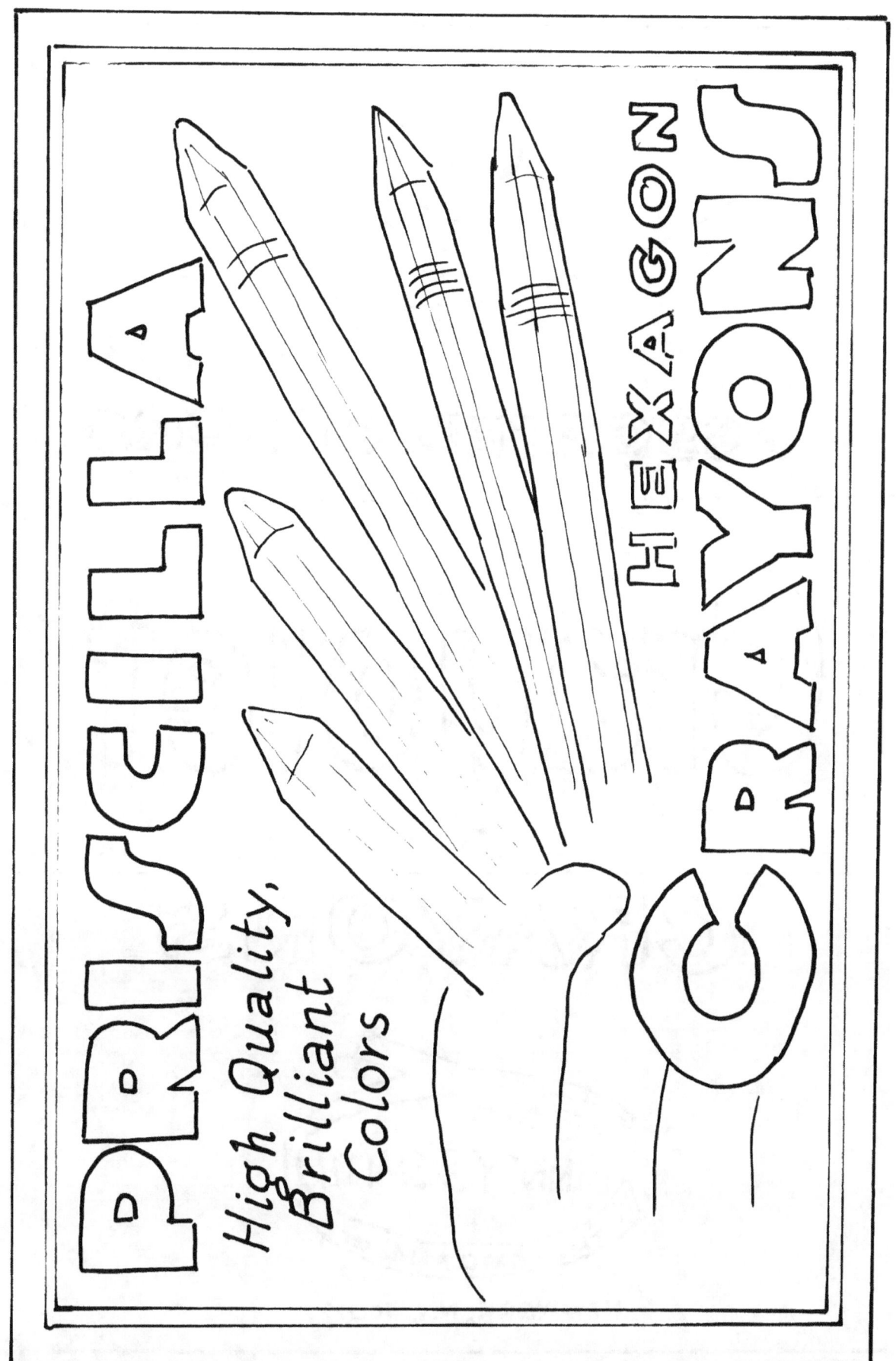

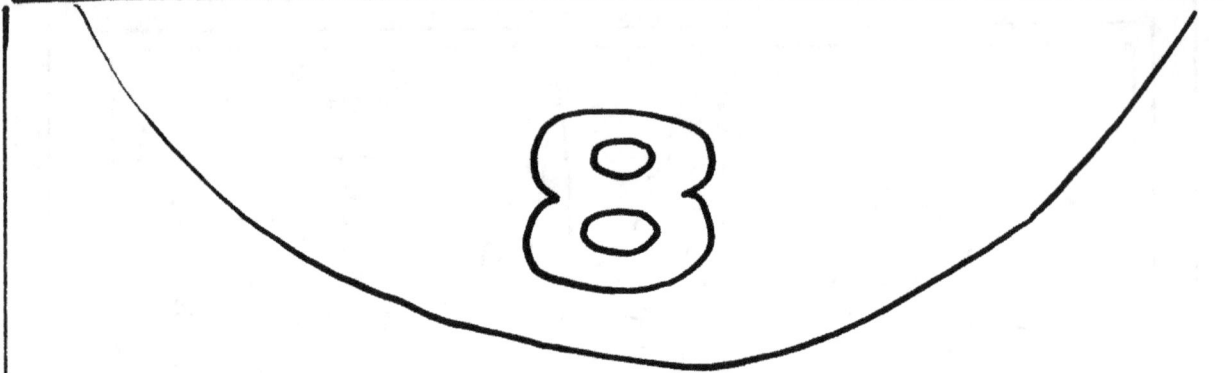

# 8

## ASSORTED COLORS

# Crayolet®

## CRAYONS

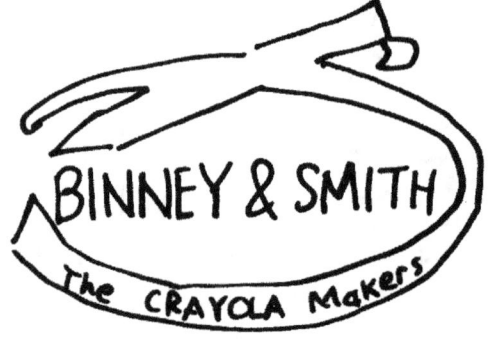

BINNEY & SMITH
The CRAYOLA Makers

NEW YORK, N.Y. 10017

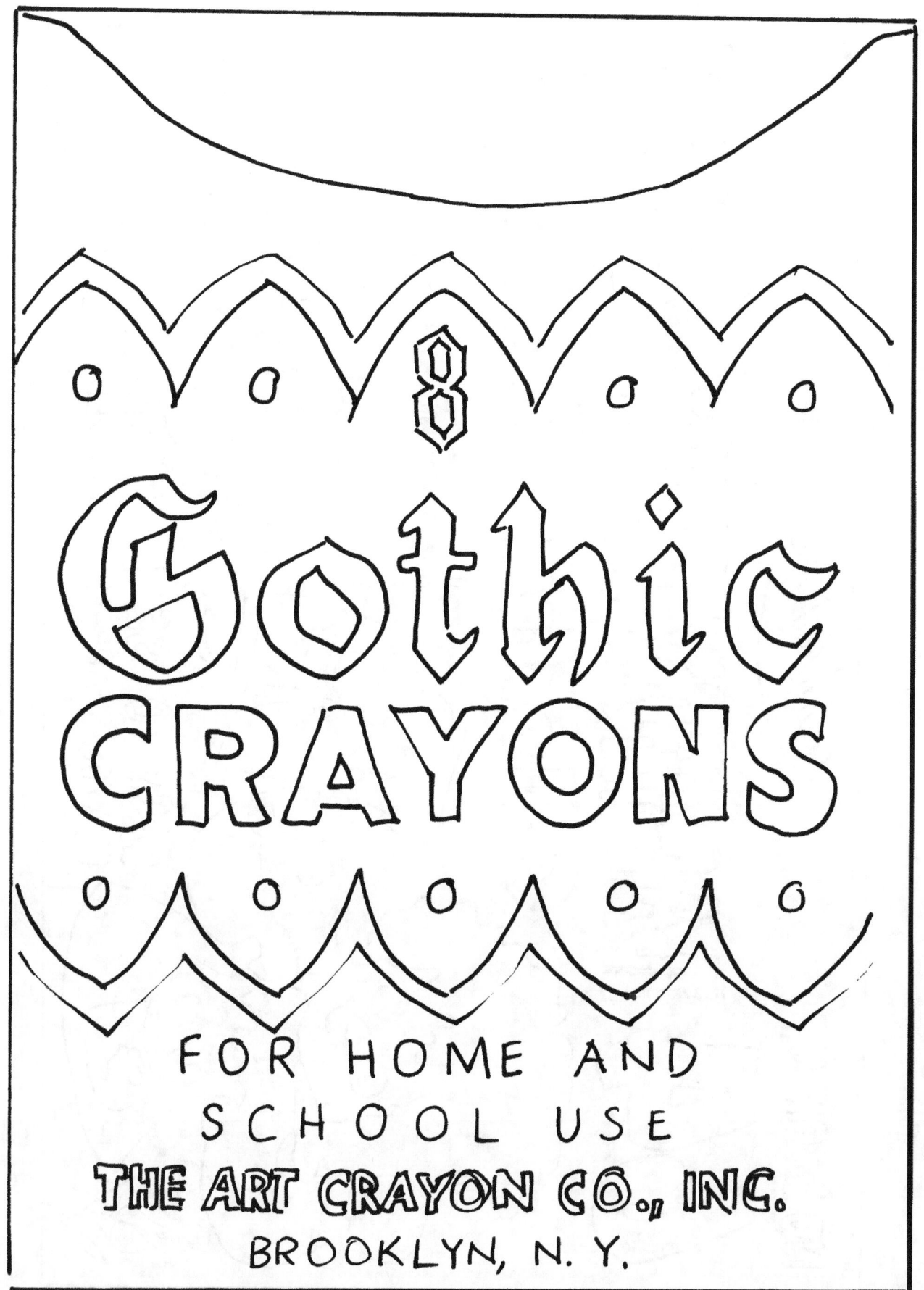

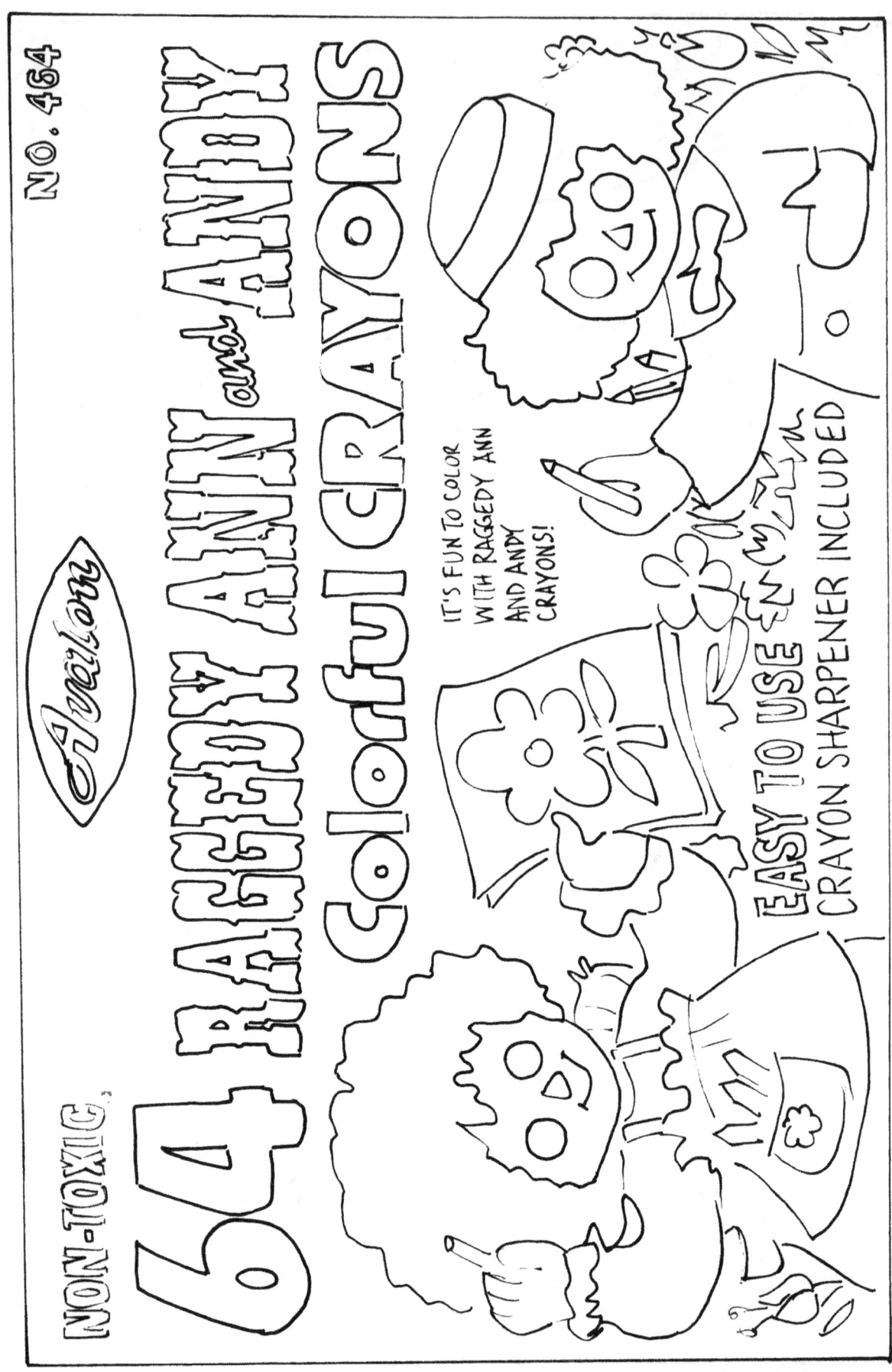

24

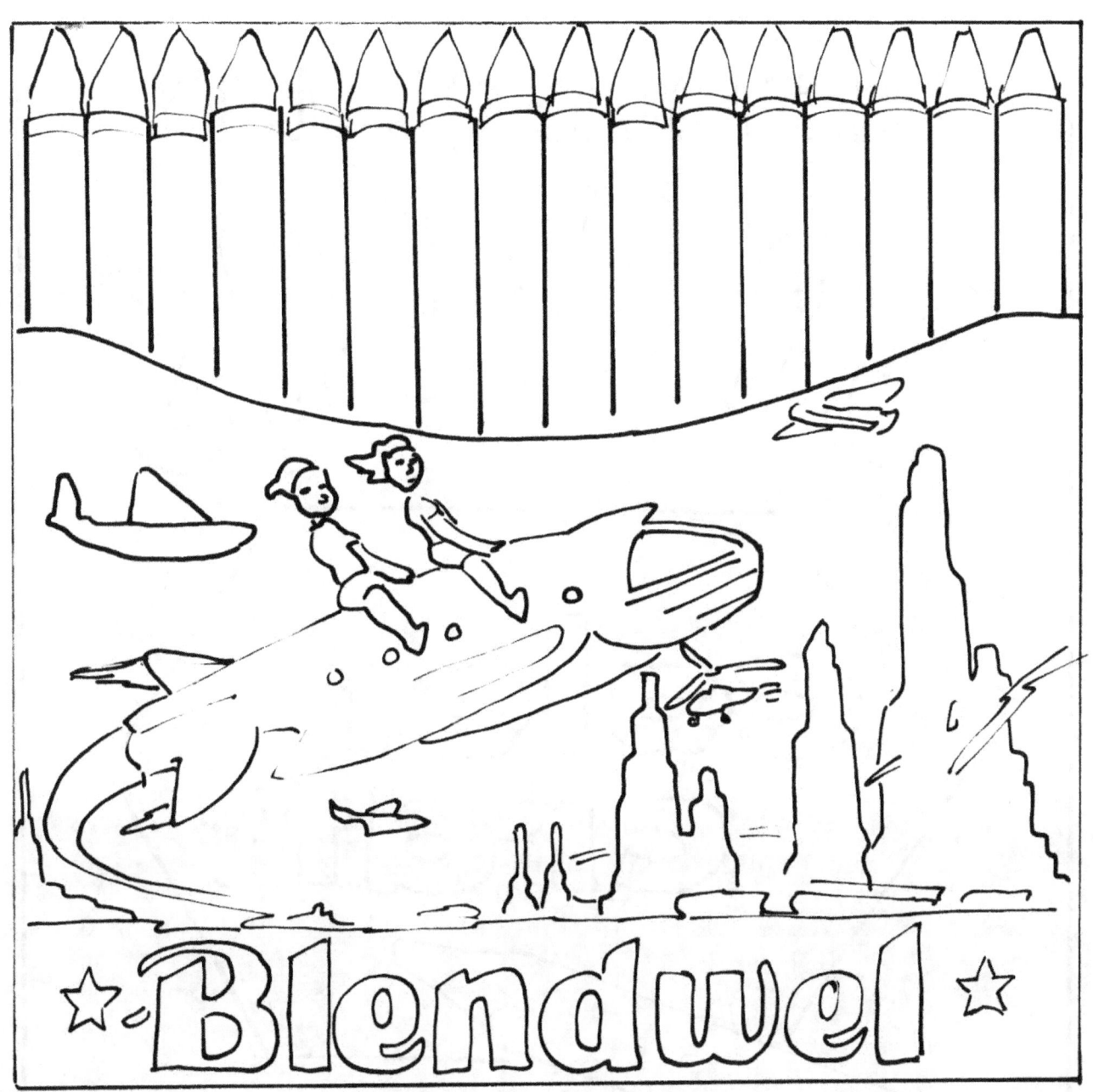

8 COLORS

SCHOOL QUALITY

CRAYONS

color craft

NON-TOXIC

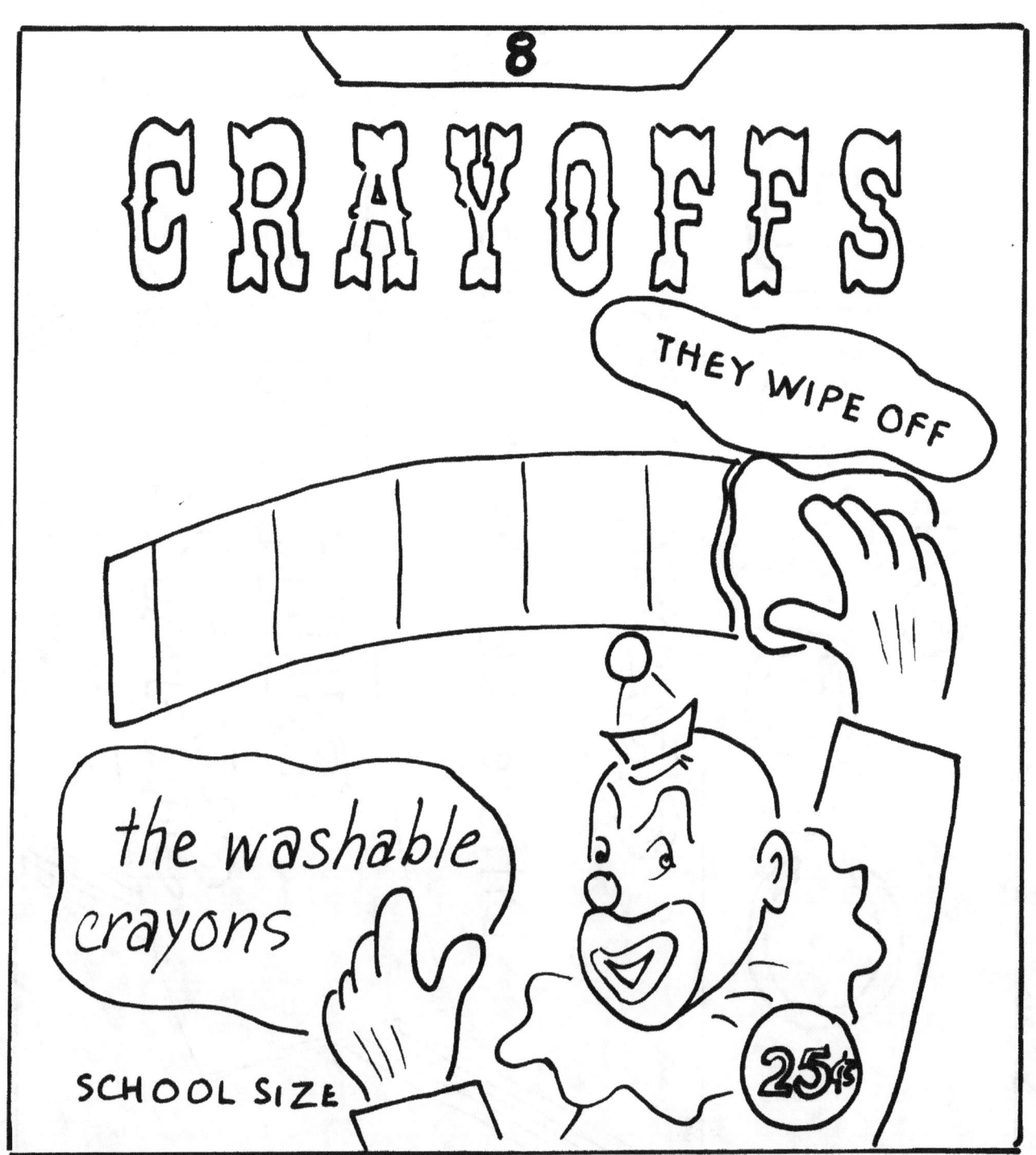

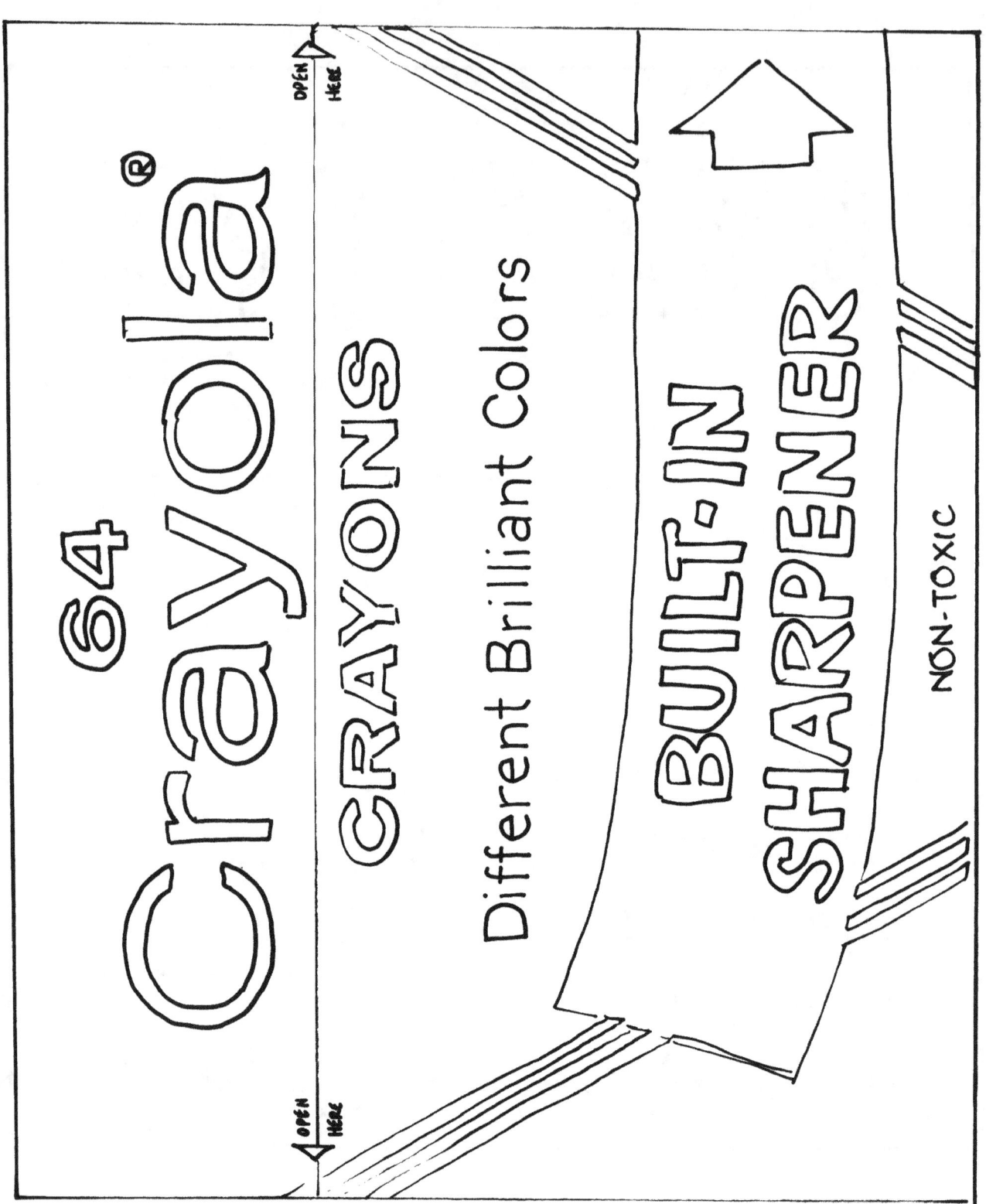

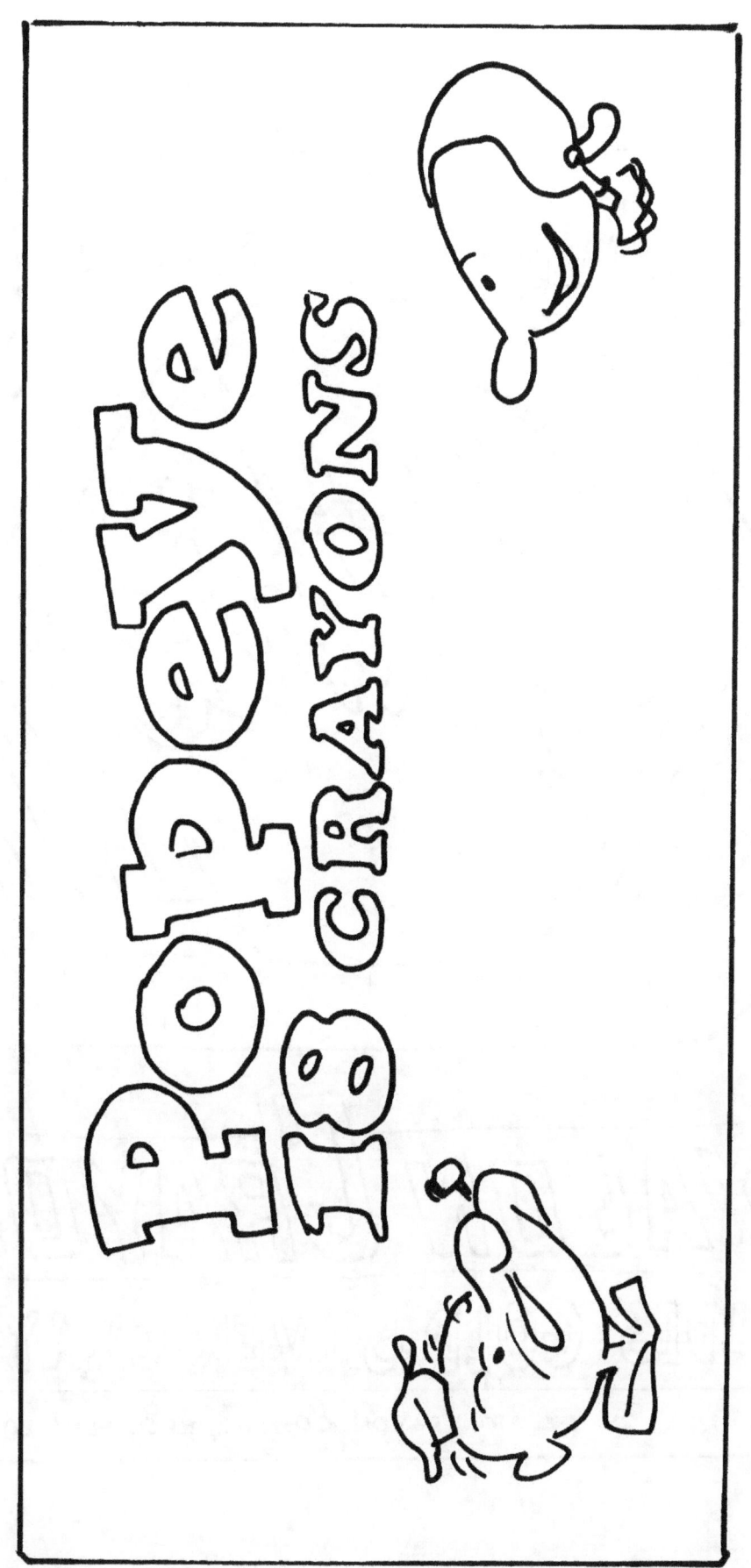

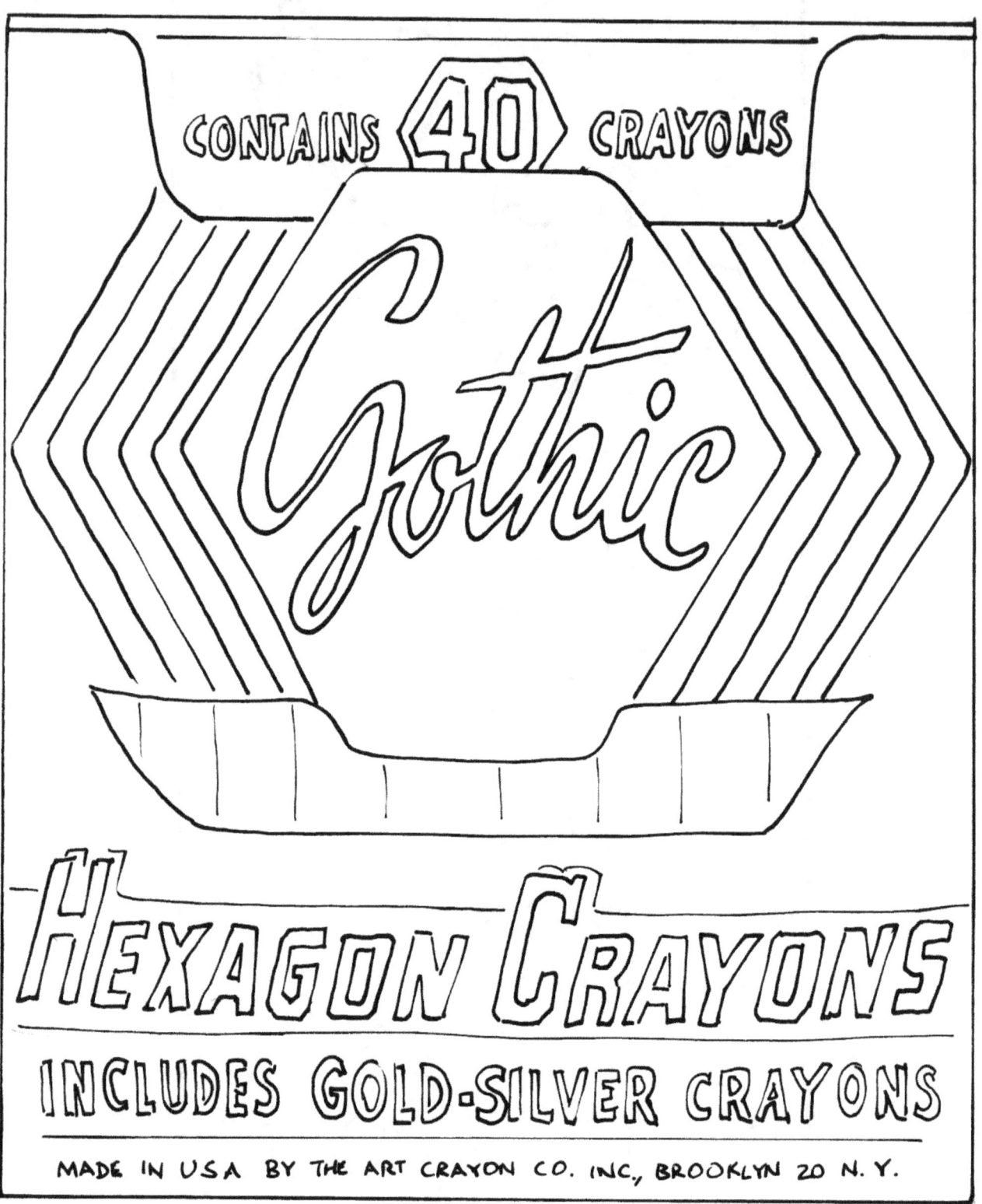

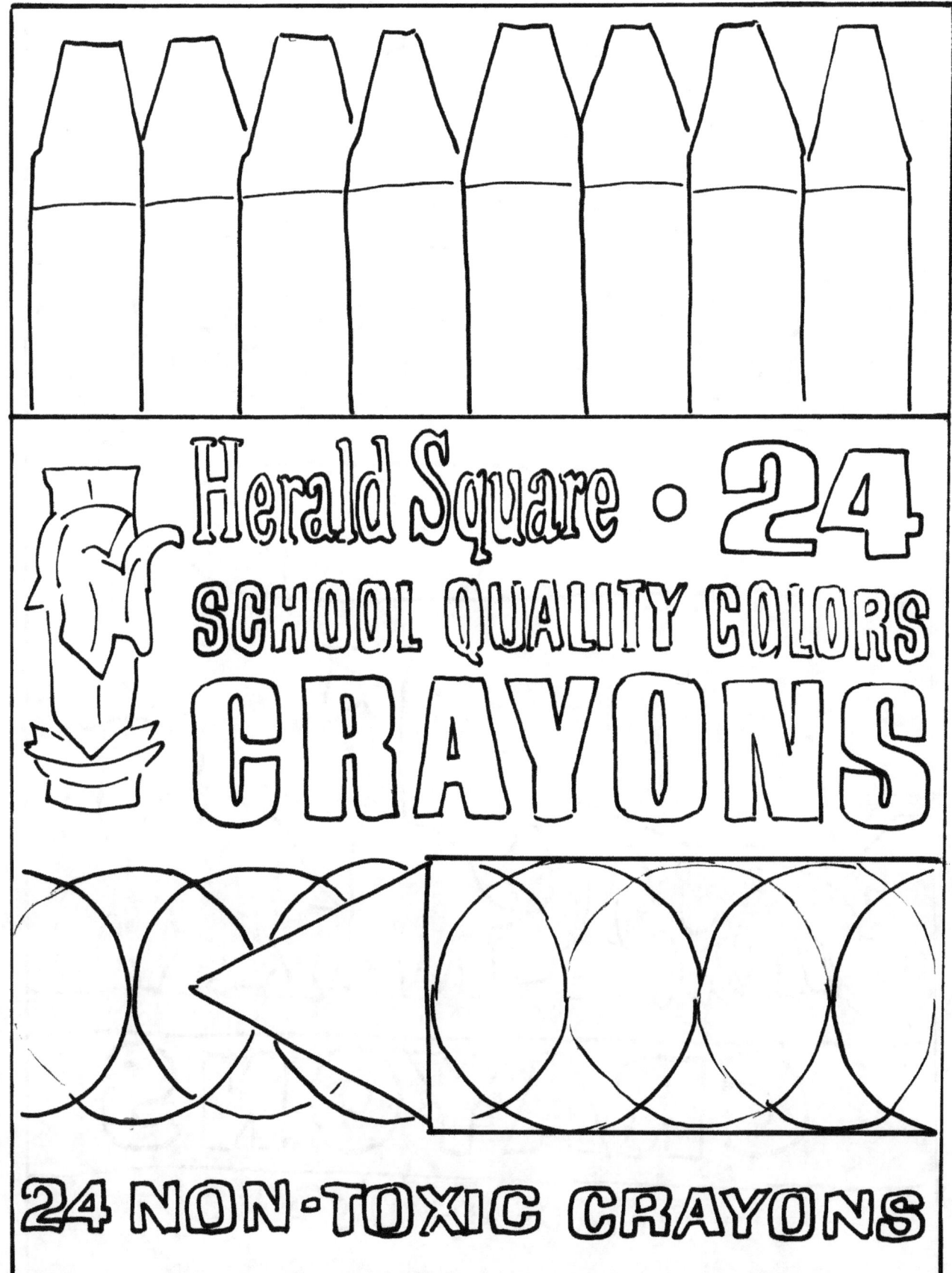

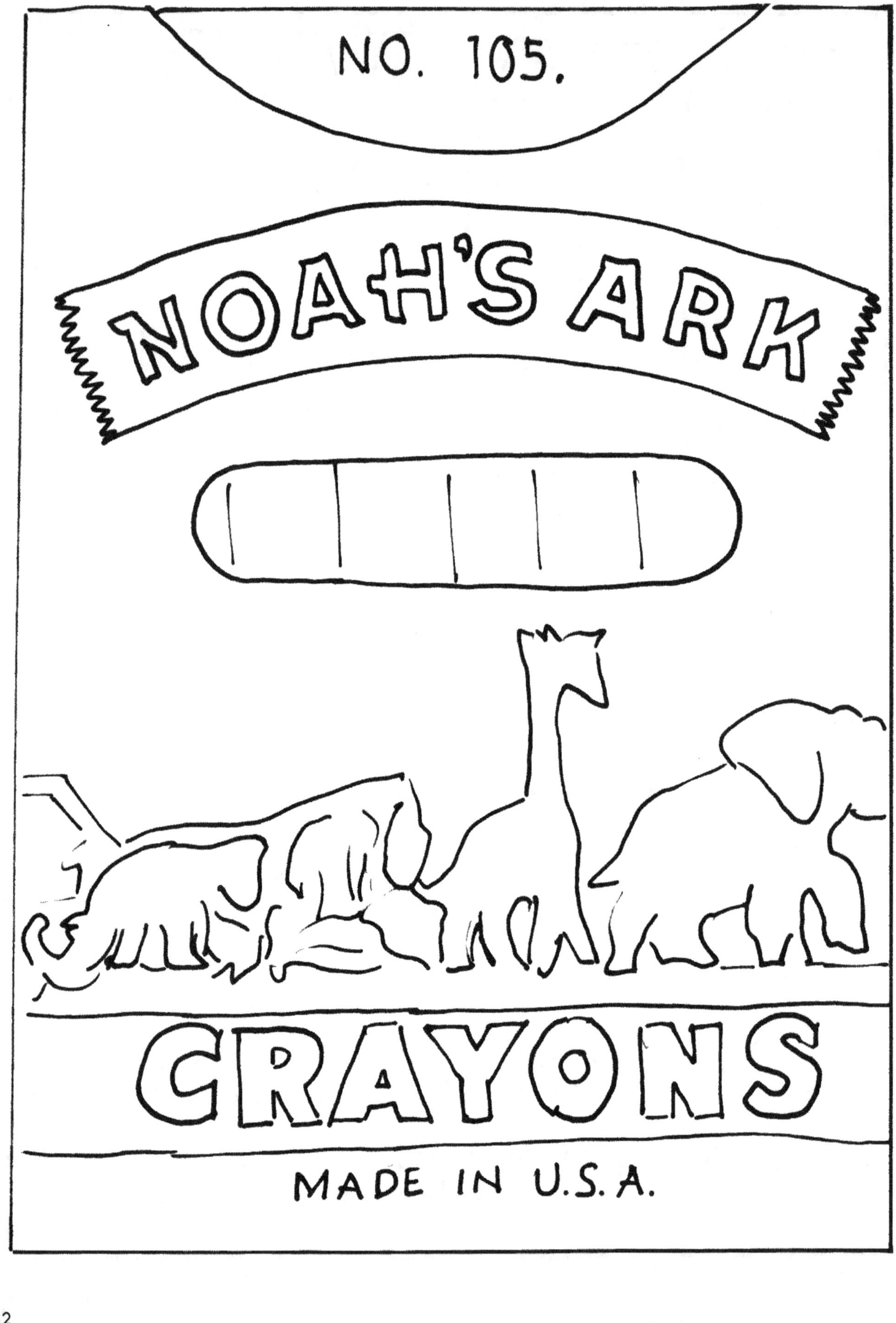

NO. 105.

NOAH'S ARK

CRAYONS

MADE IN U.S.A.

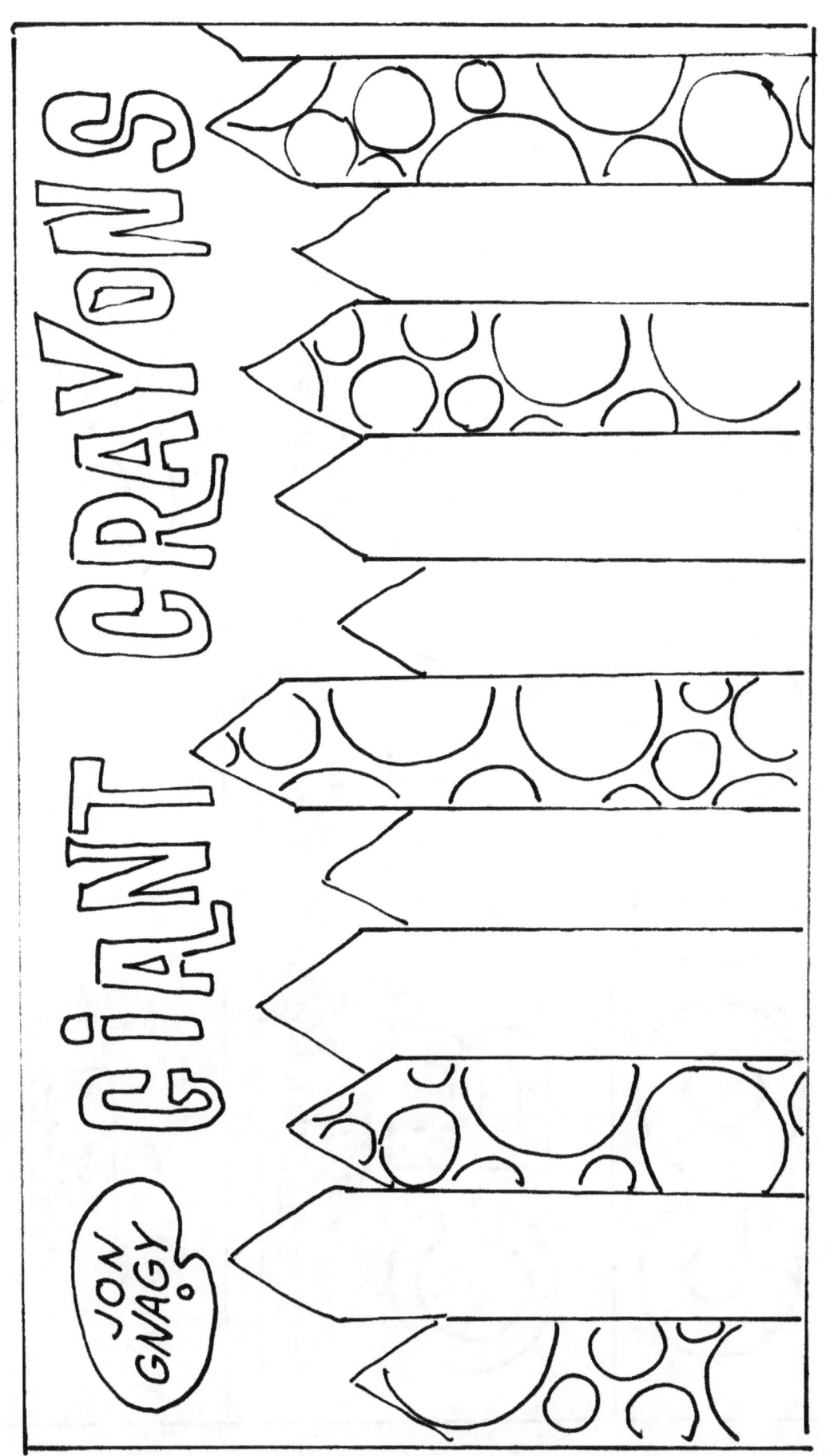

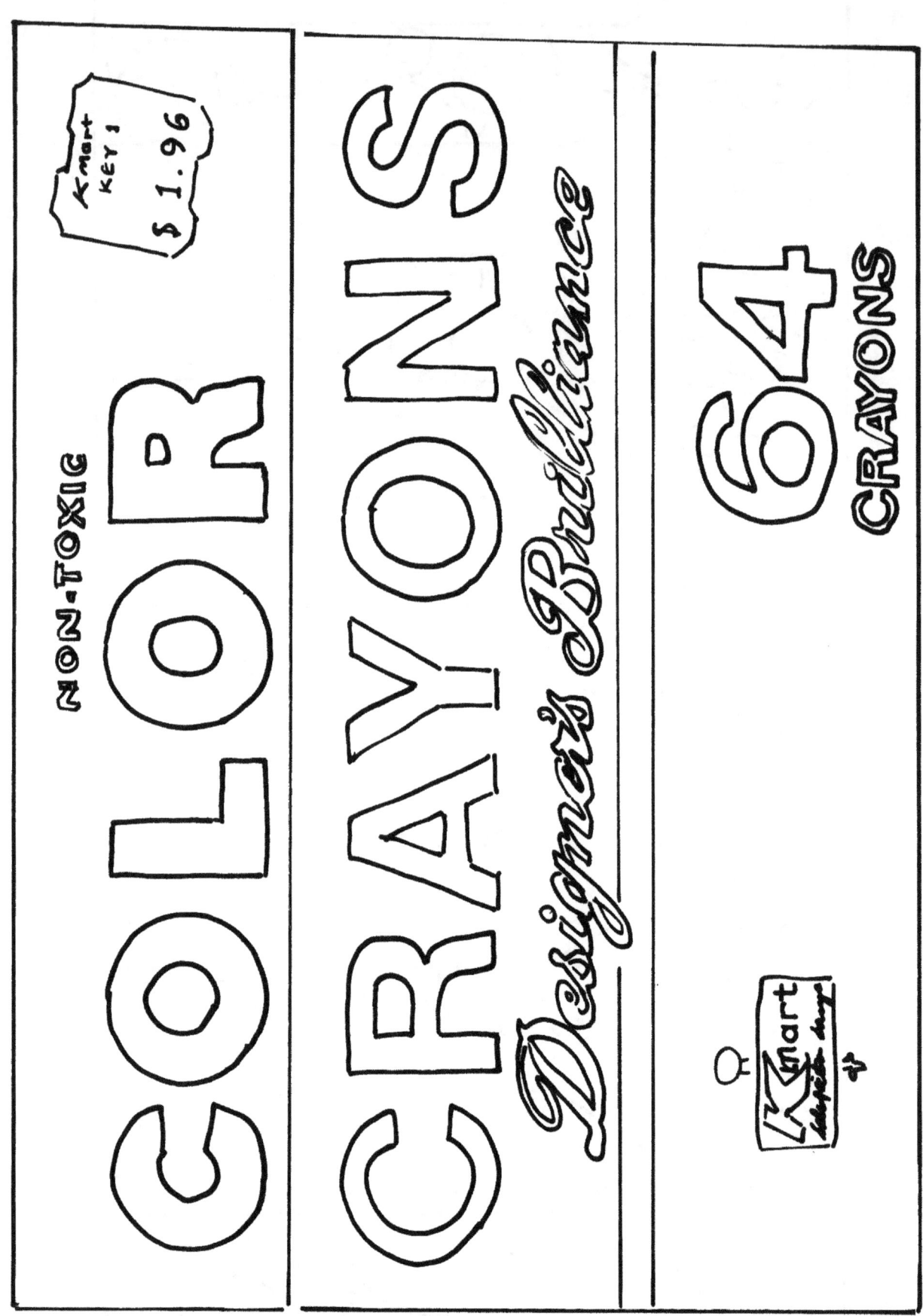

NON-TOXIC

COLOR

CRAYONS

Designer's Brilliance

64

CRAYONS

K-mart
KEY 1
$1.96

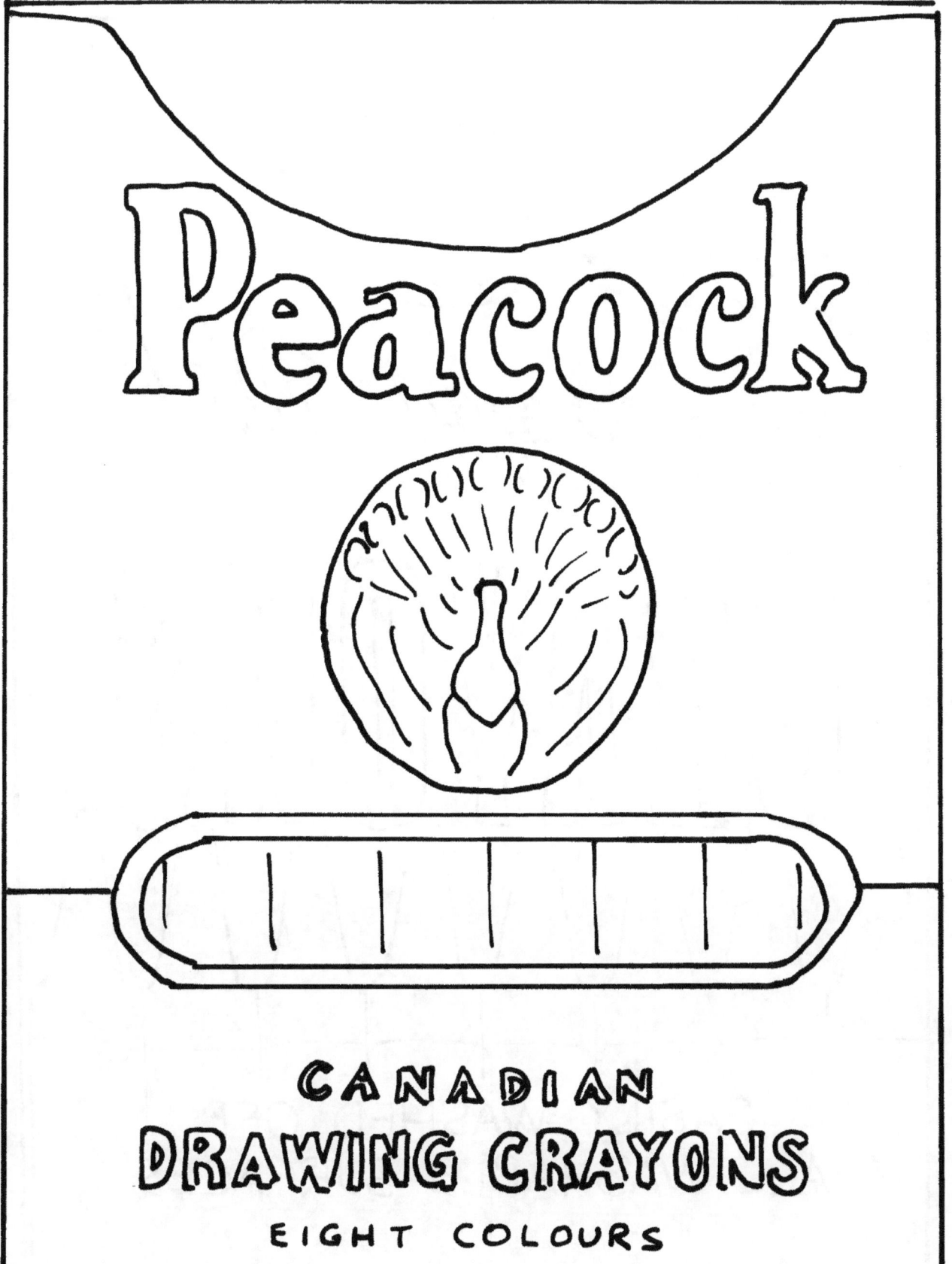

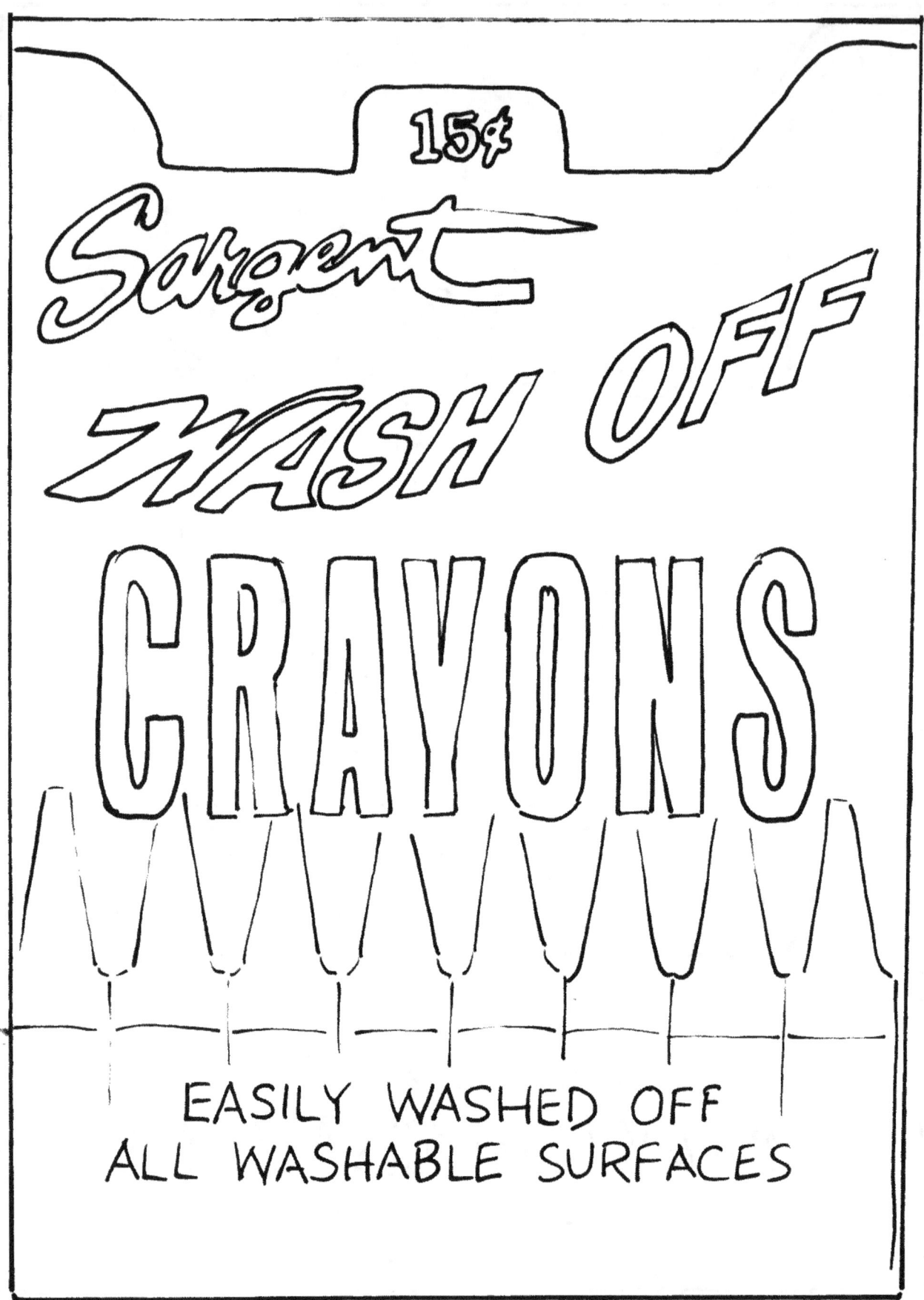

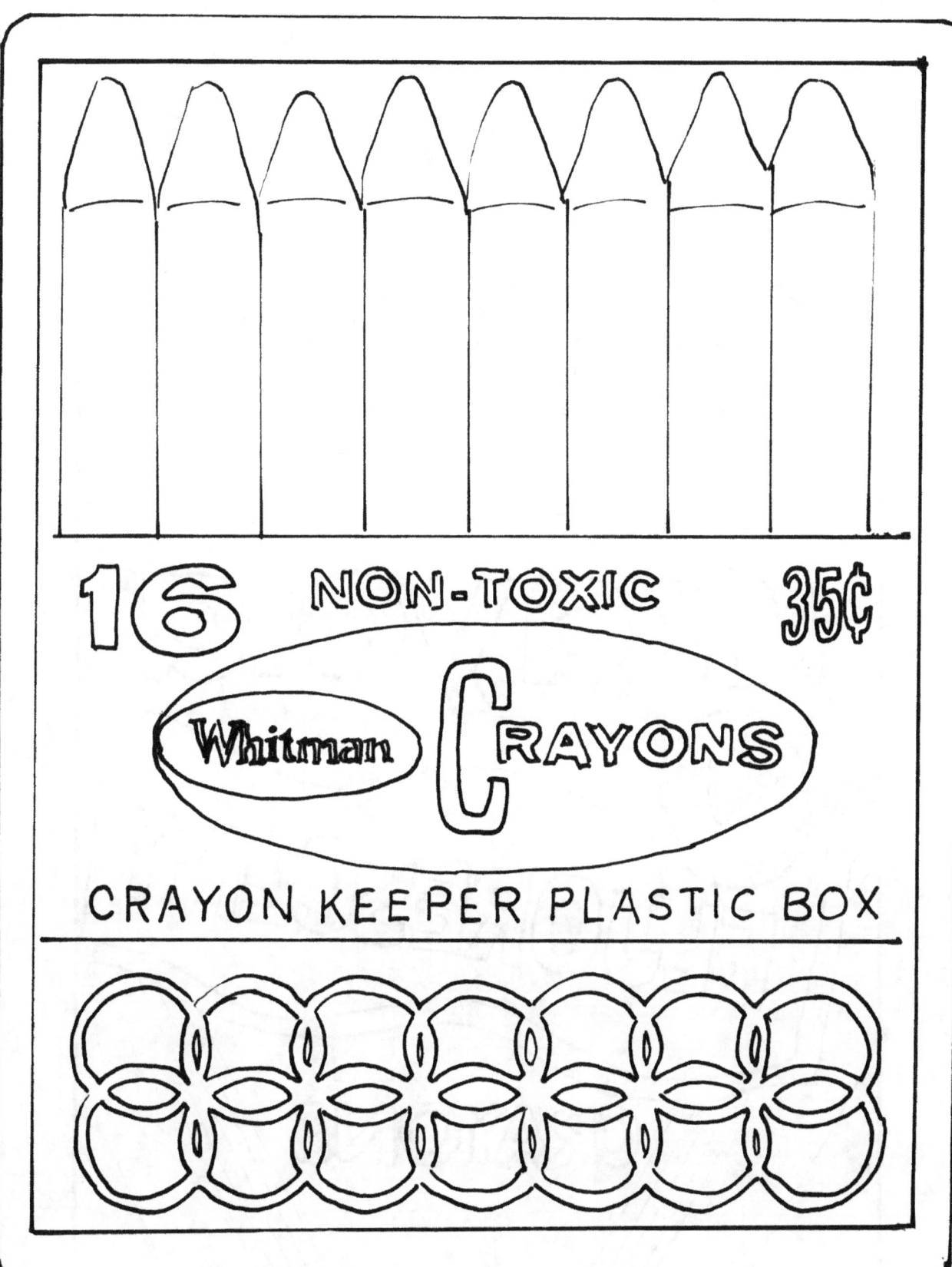

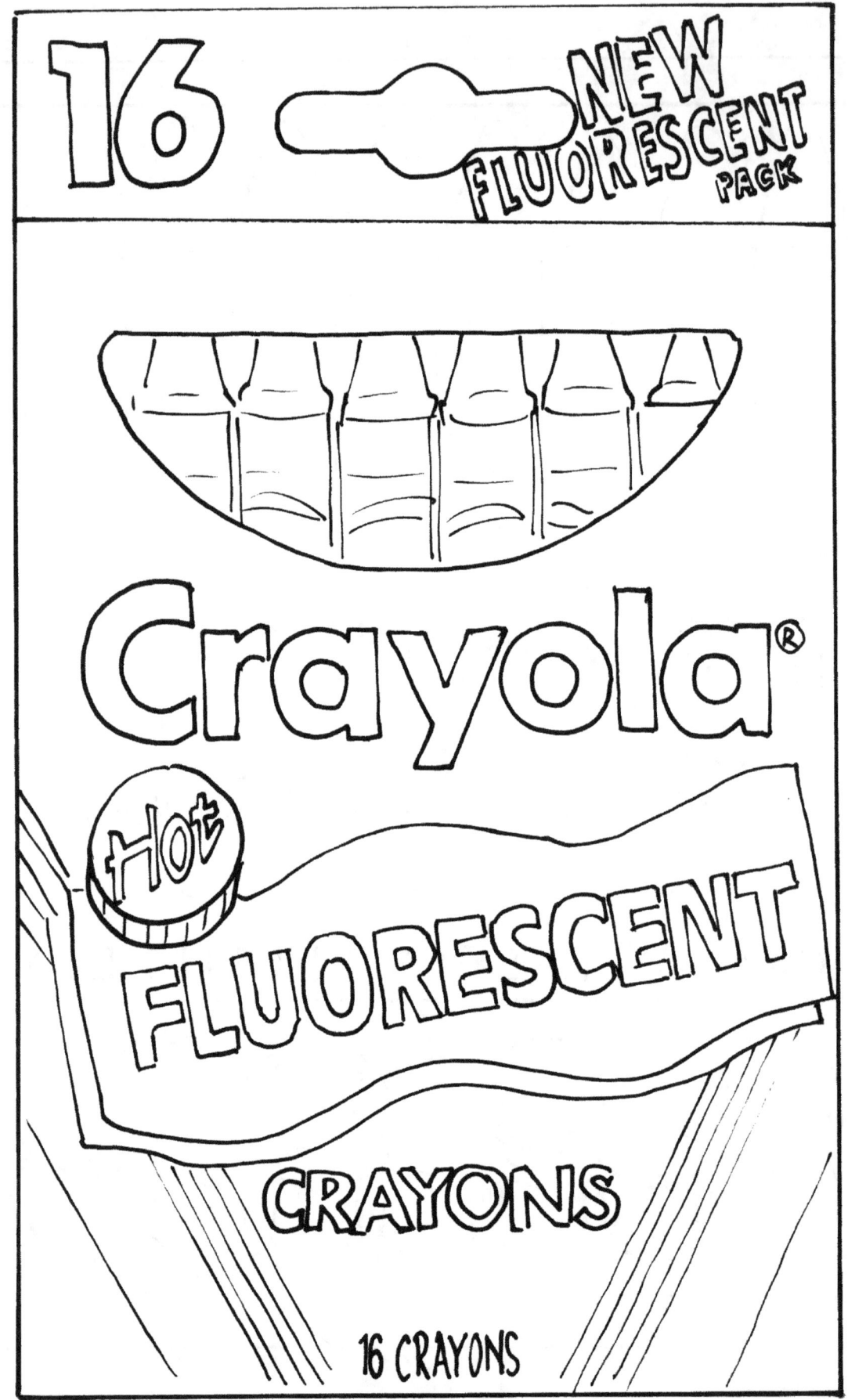

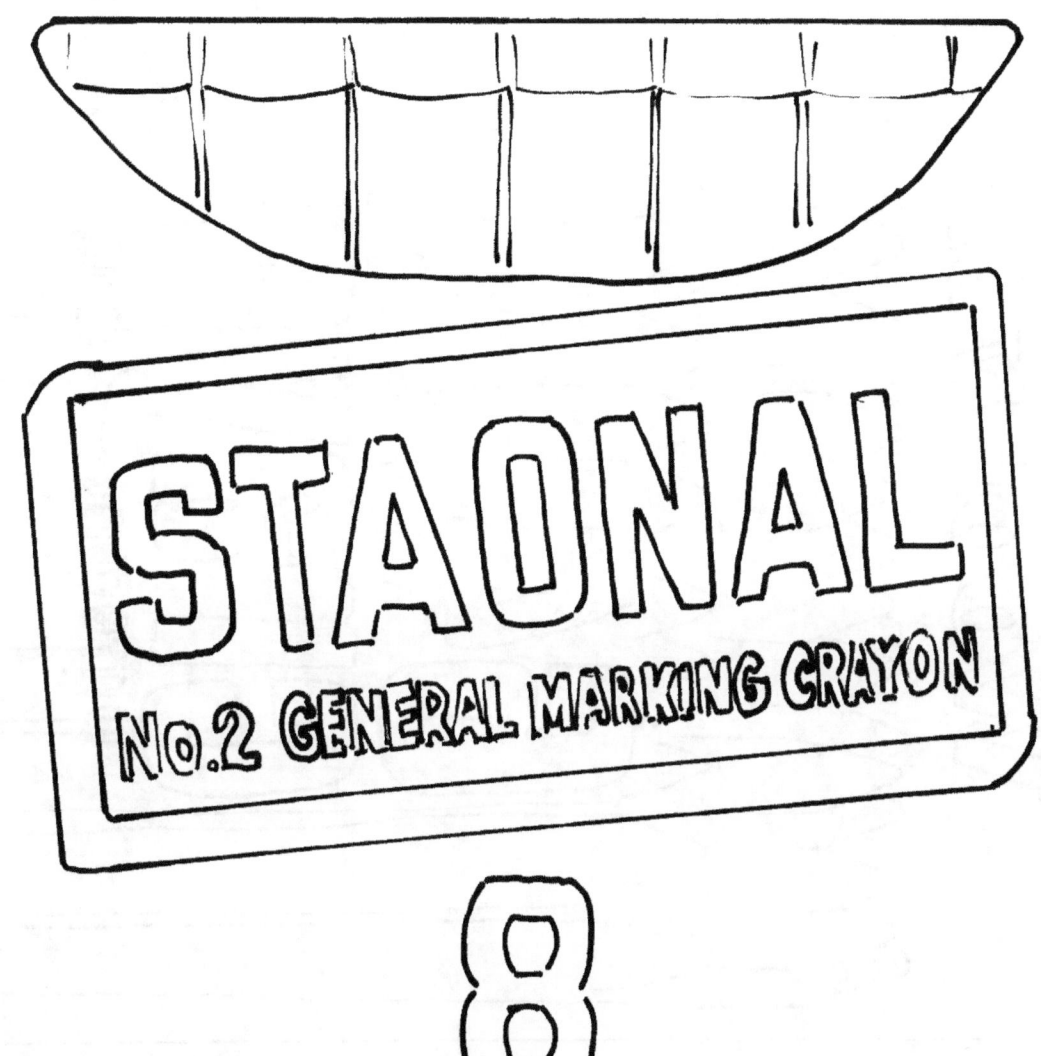

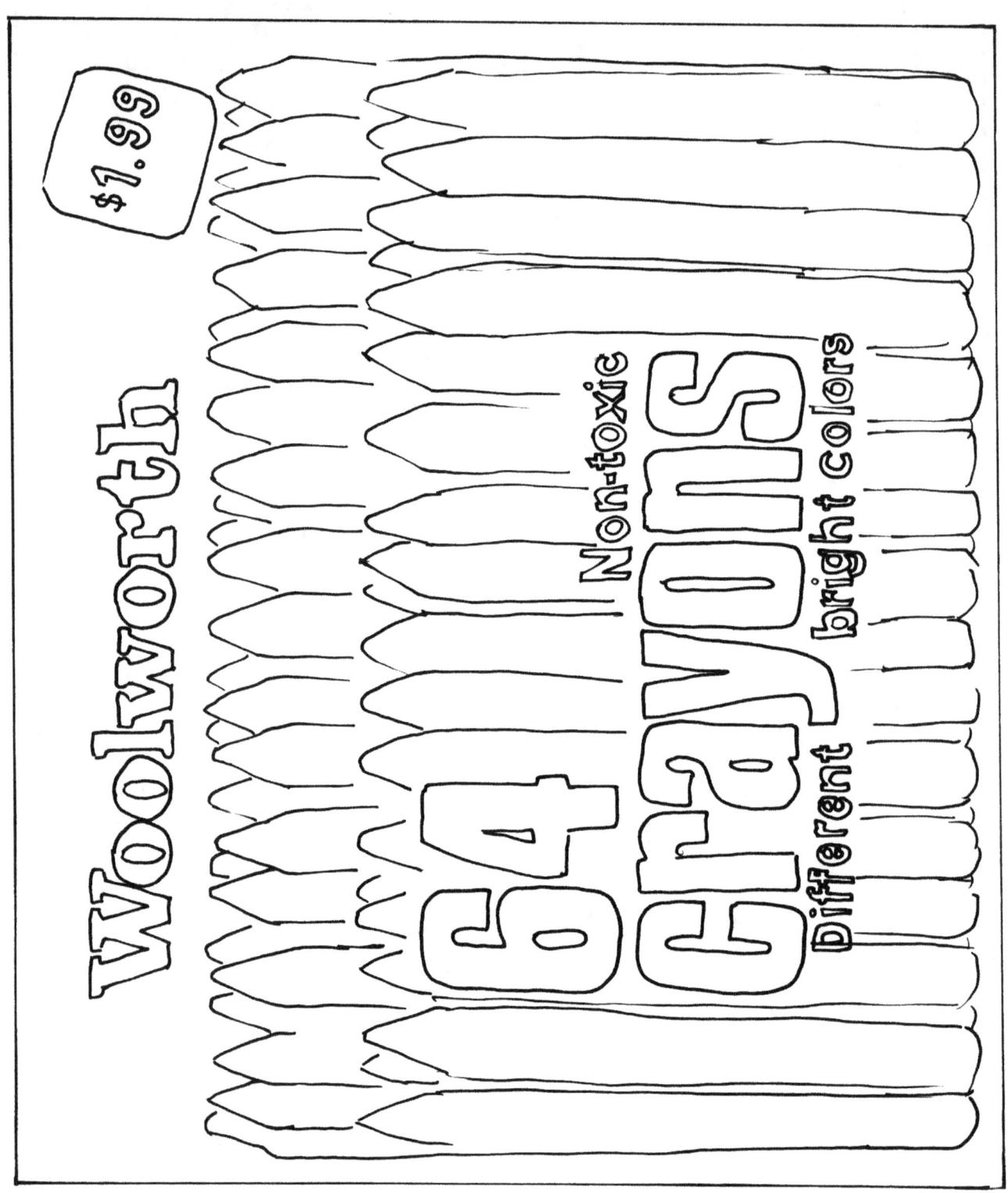

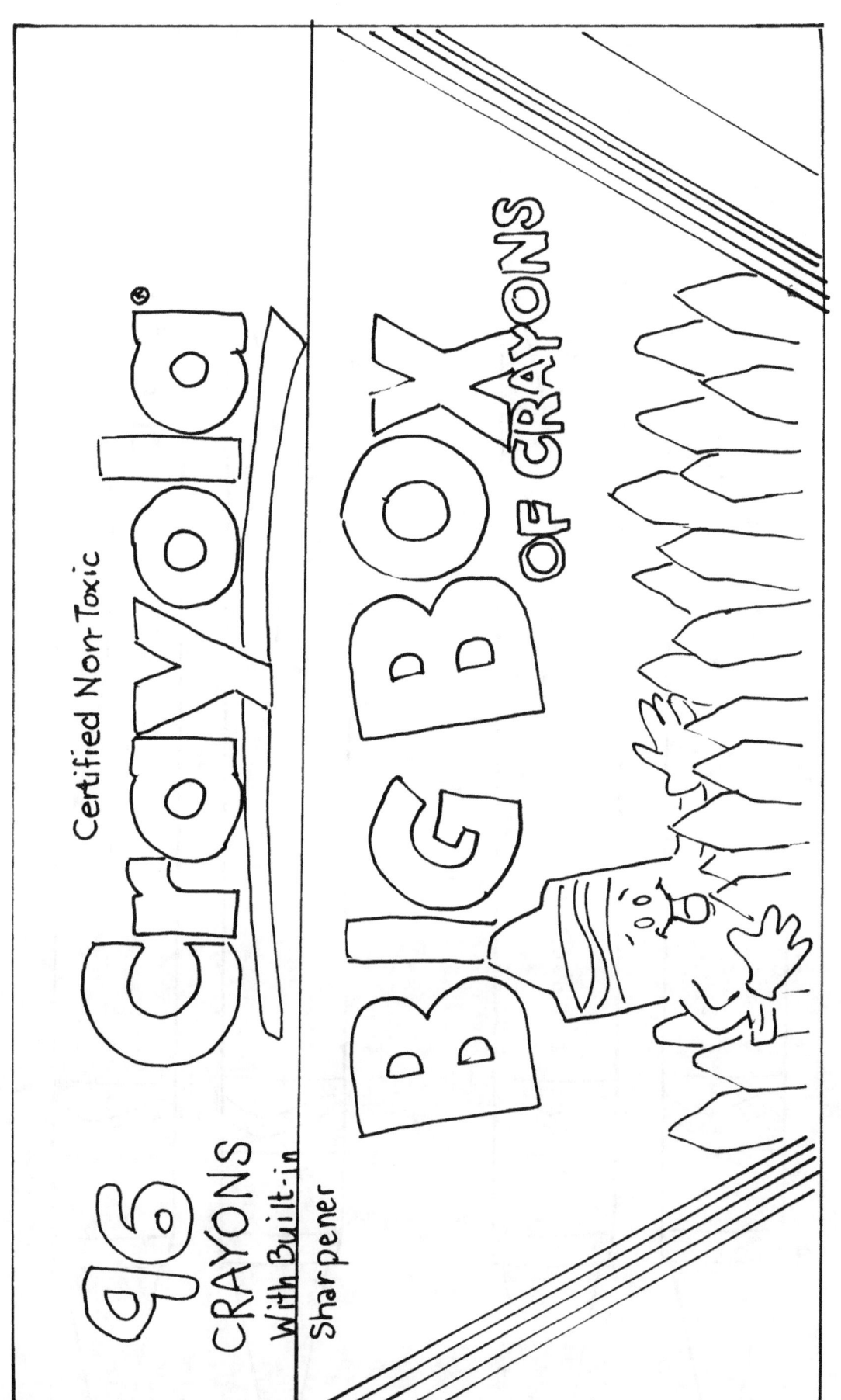

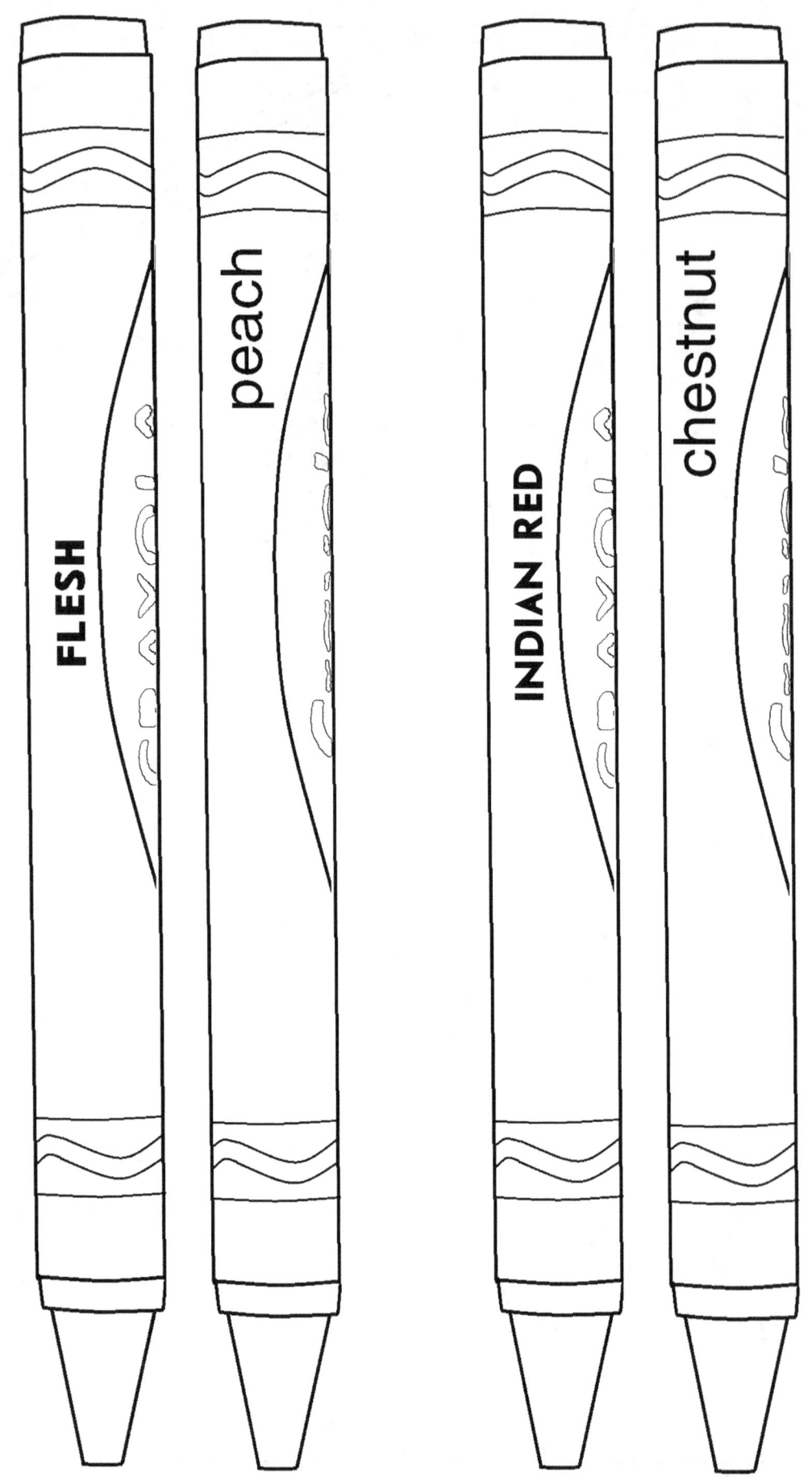

FLESH

peach

INDIAN RED

chestnut

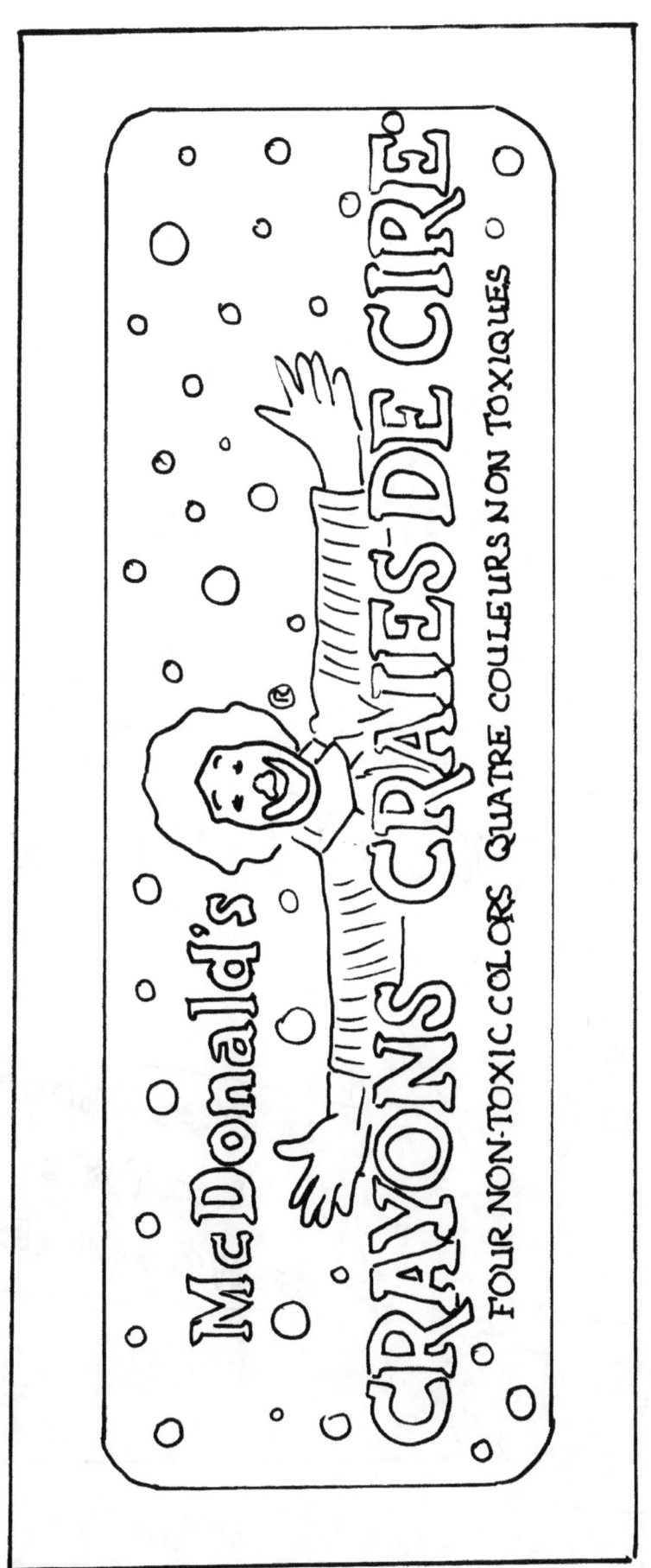

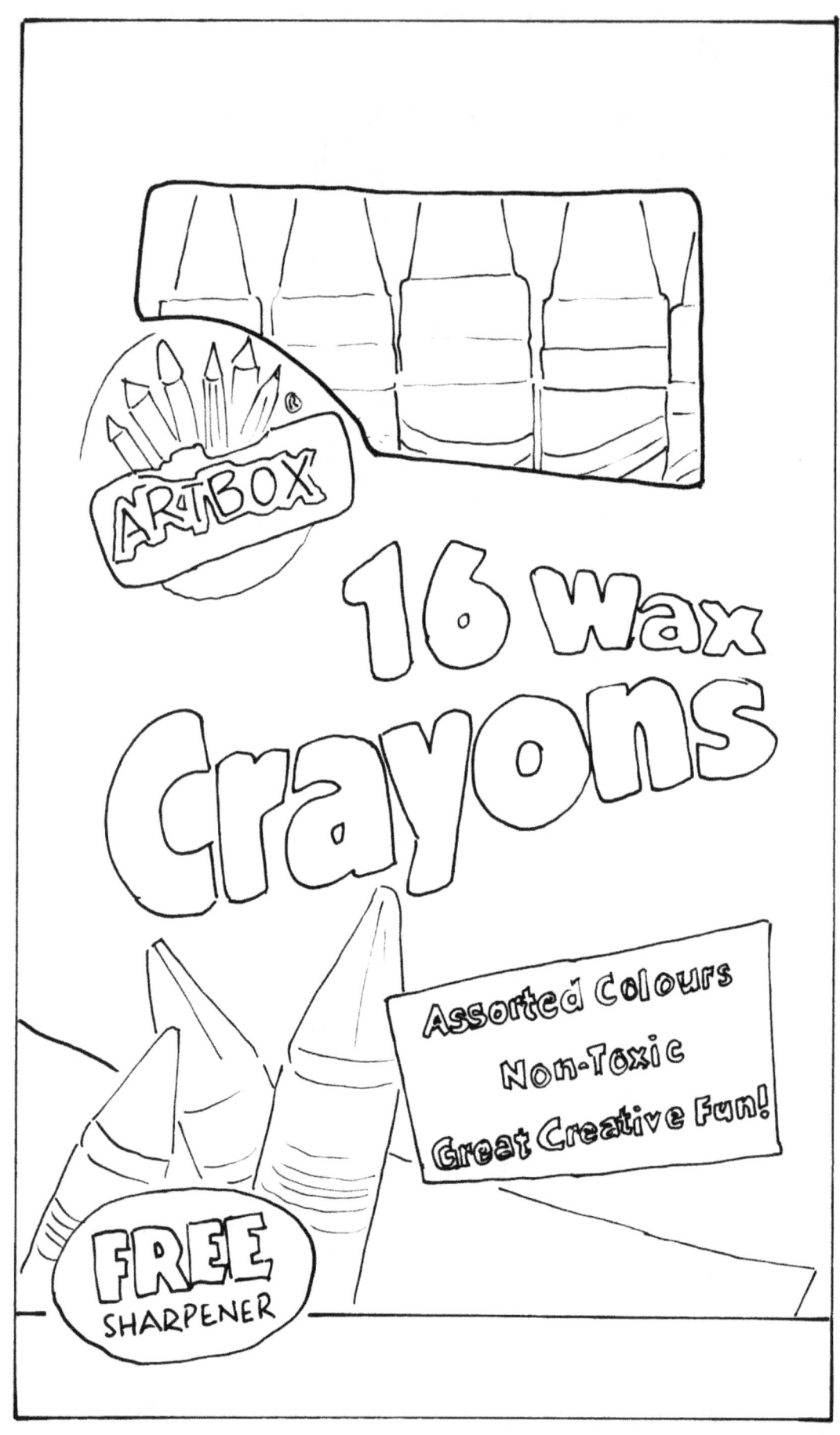

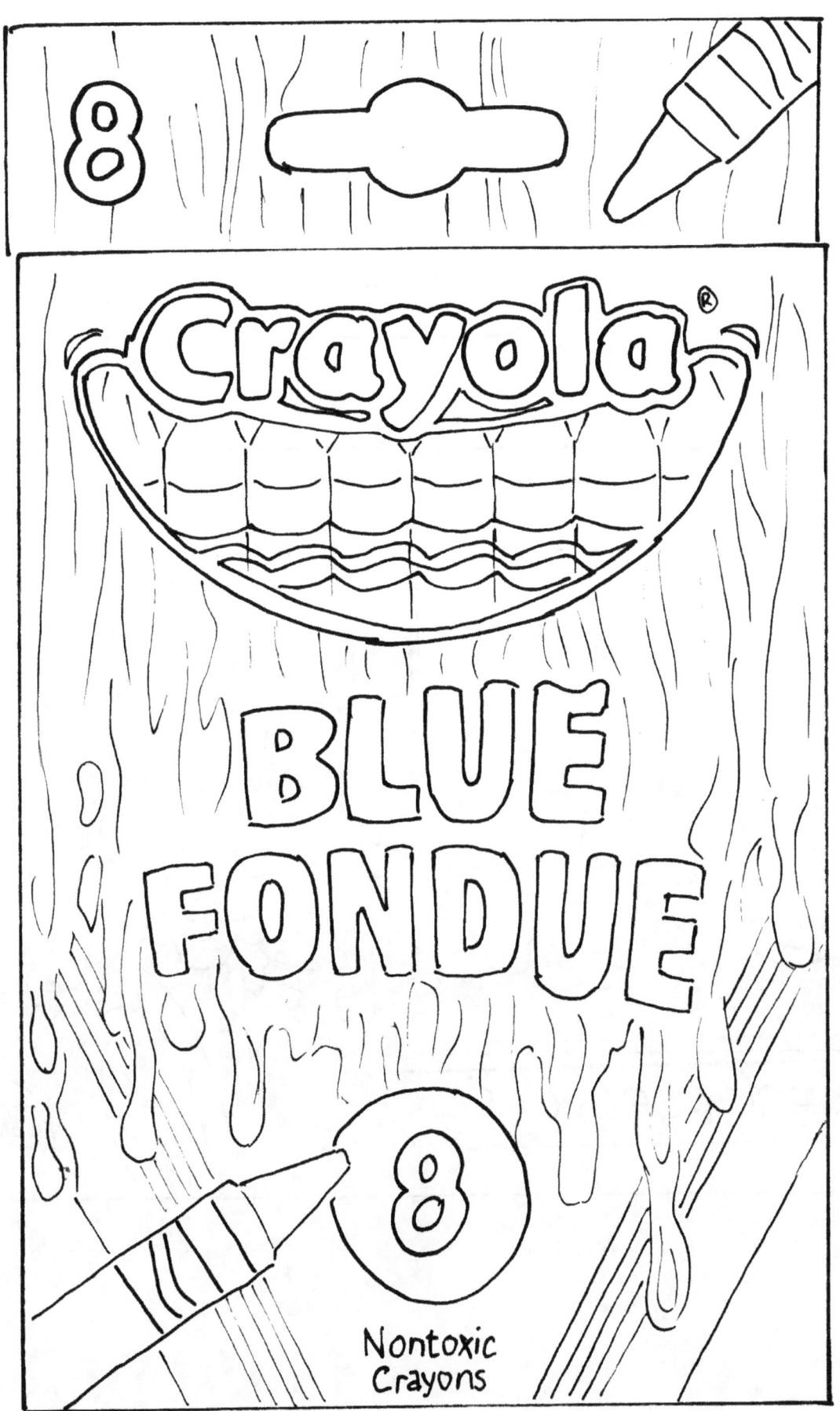

8

Crayola®

BLUE
FONDUE

8

Nontoxic
Crayons

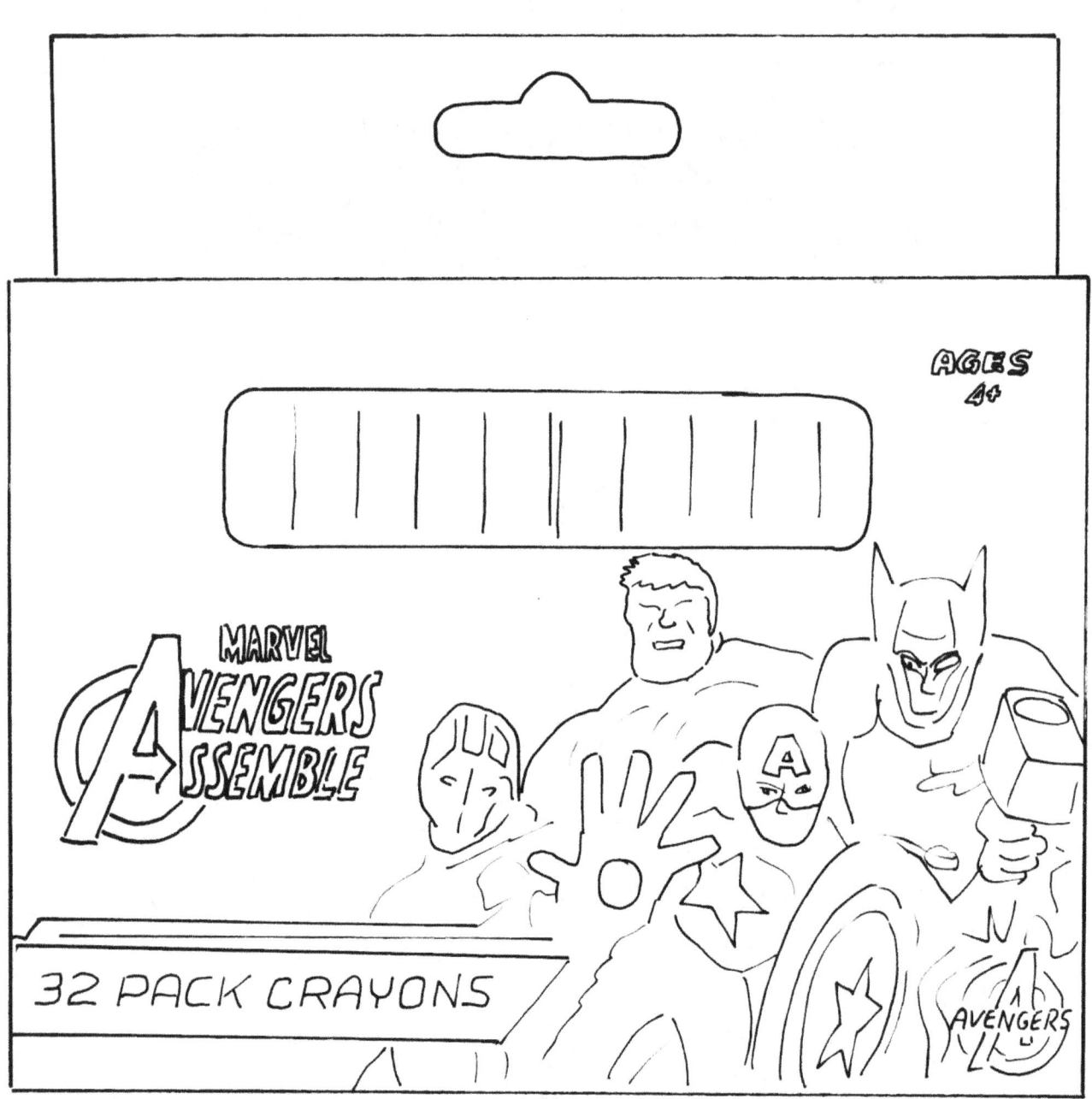

AGES
4+

MARVEL
AVENGERS
ASSEMBLE

32 PACK CRAYONS

AVENGERS

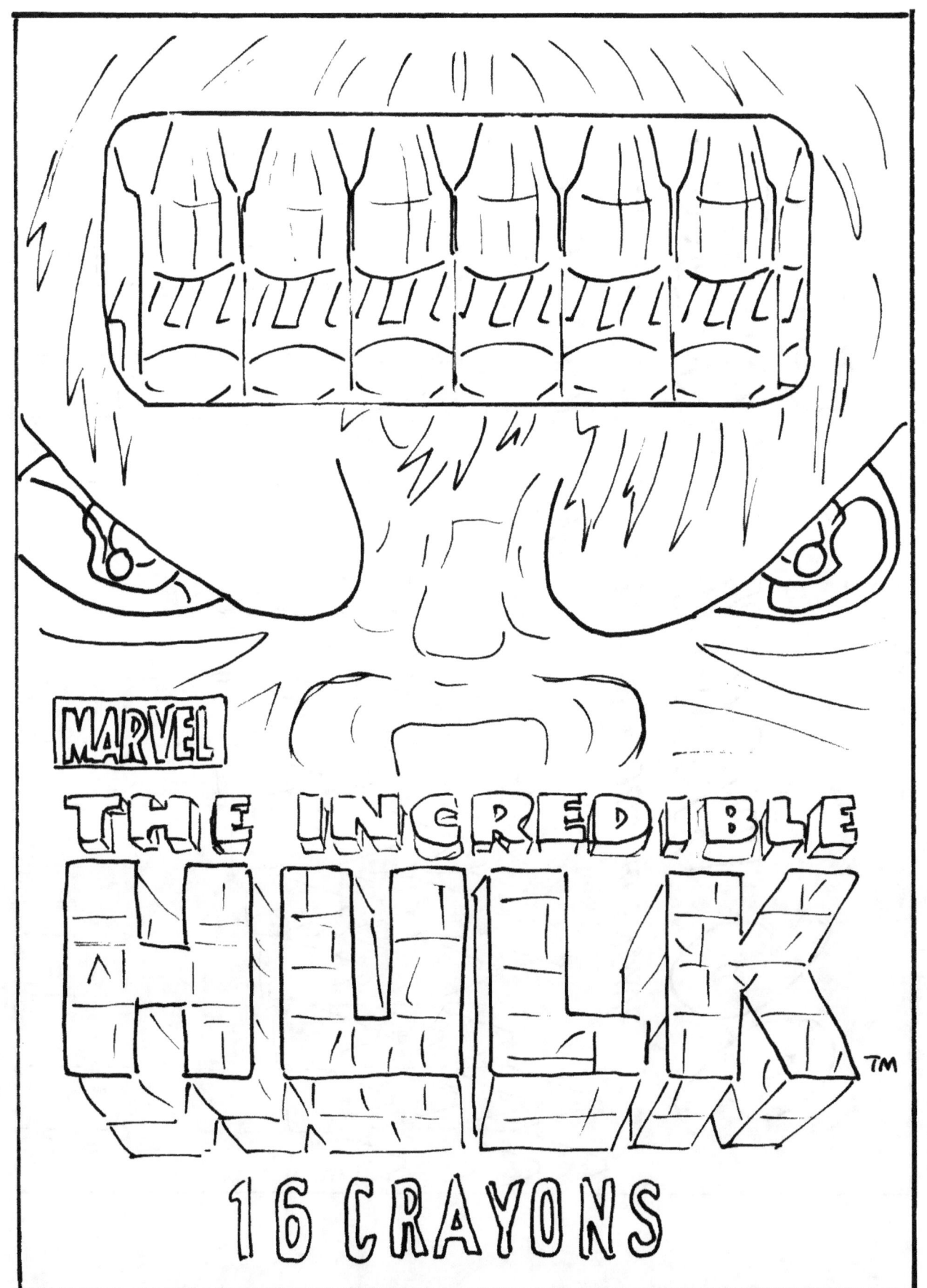

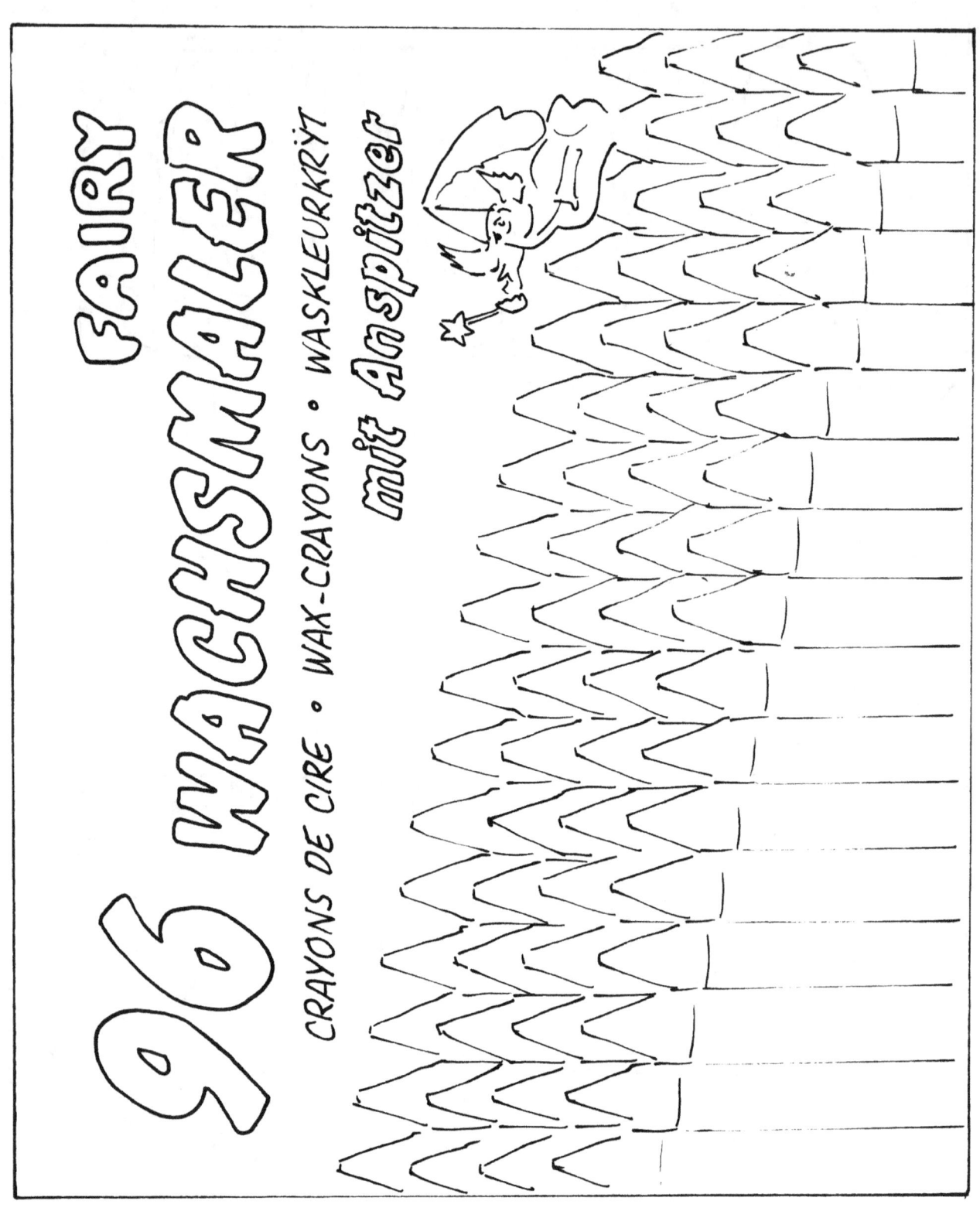

FAIRY

96 WACHSMALER

CRAYONS DE CIRE • WAX-CRAYONS • WASKLEURKRYT

mit Anspitzer

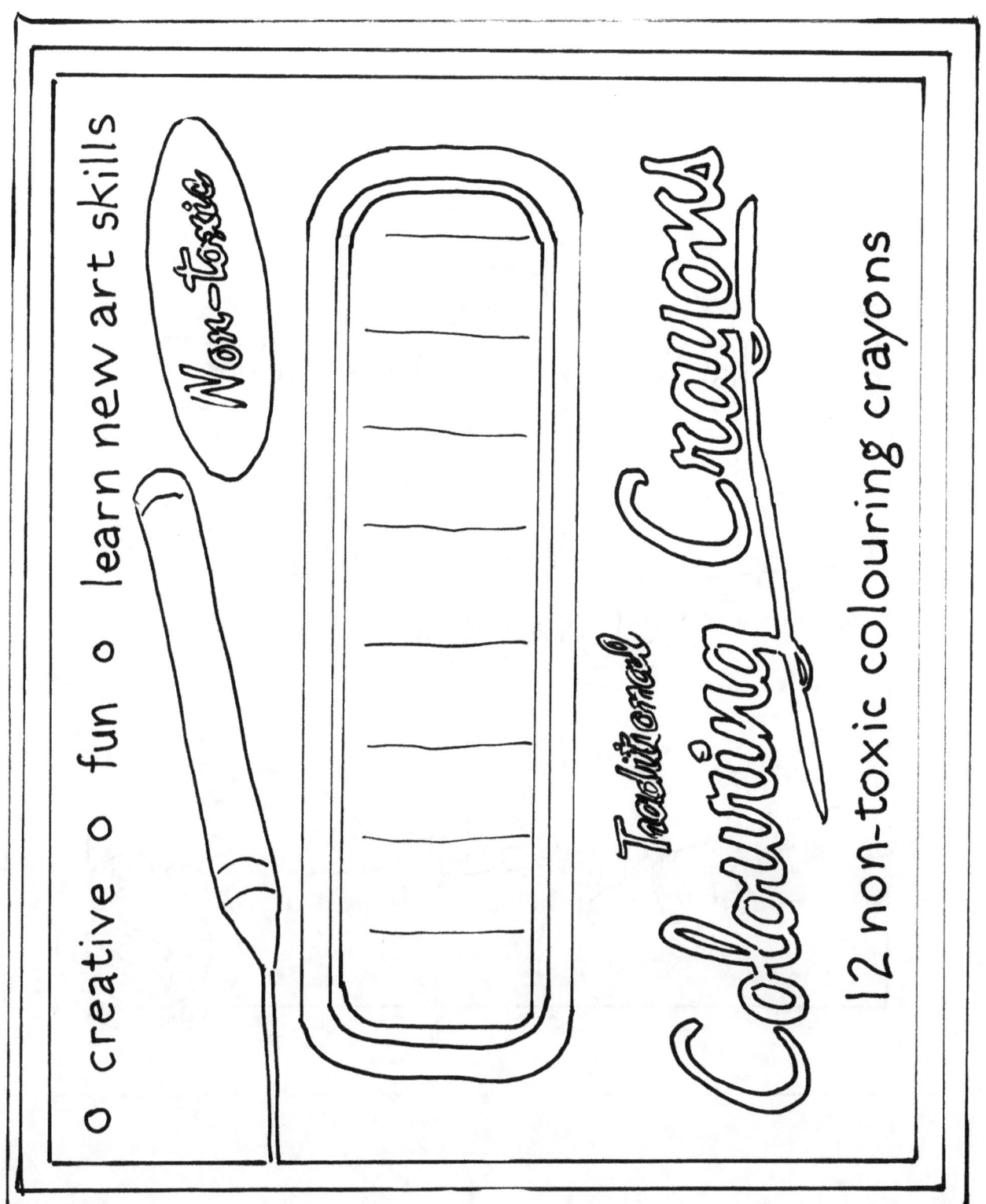

49

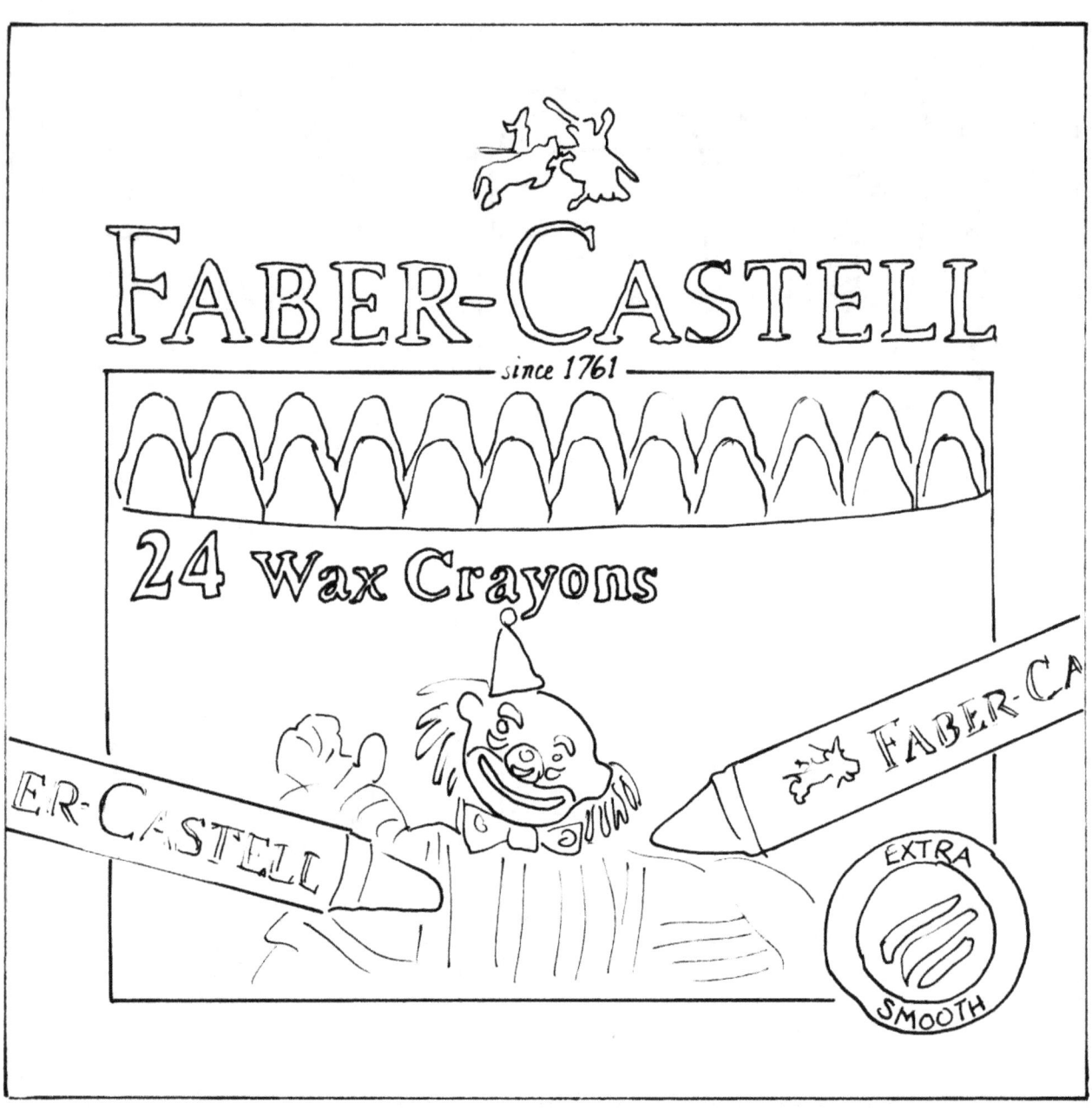

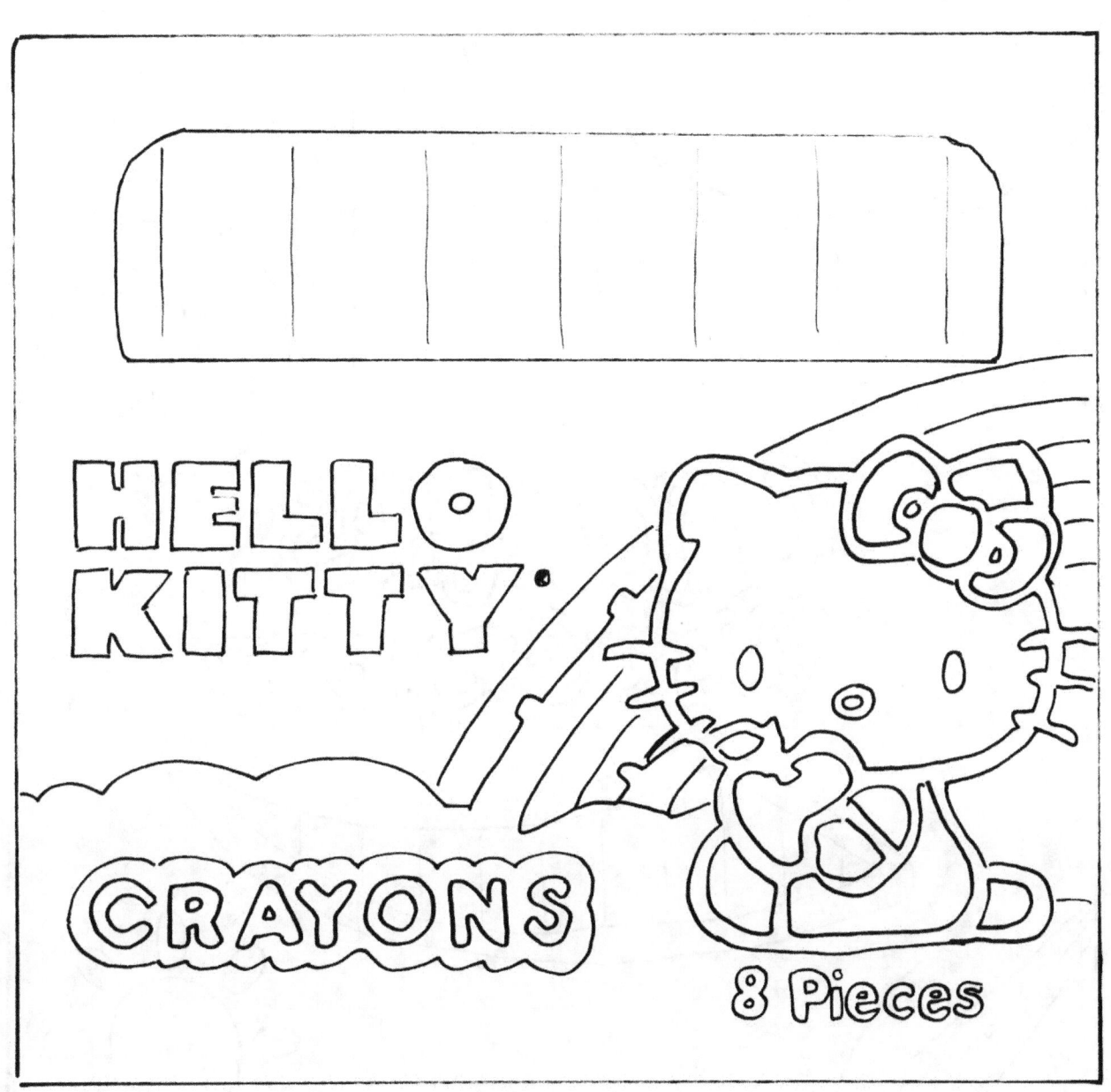

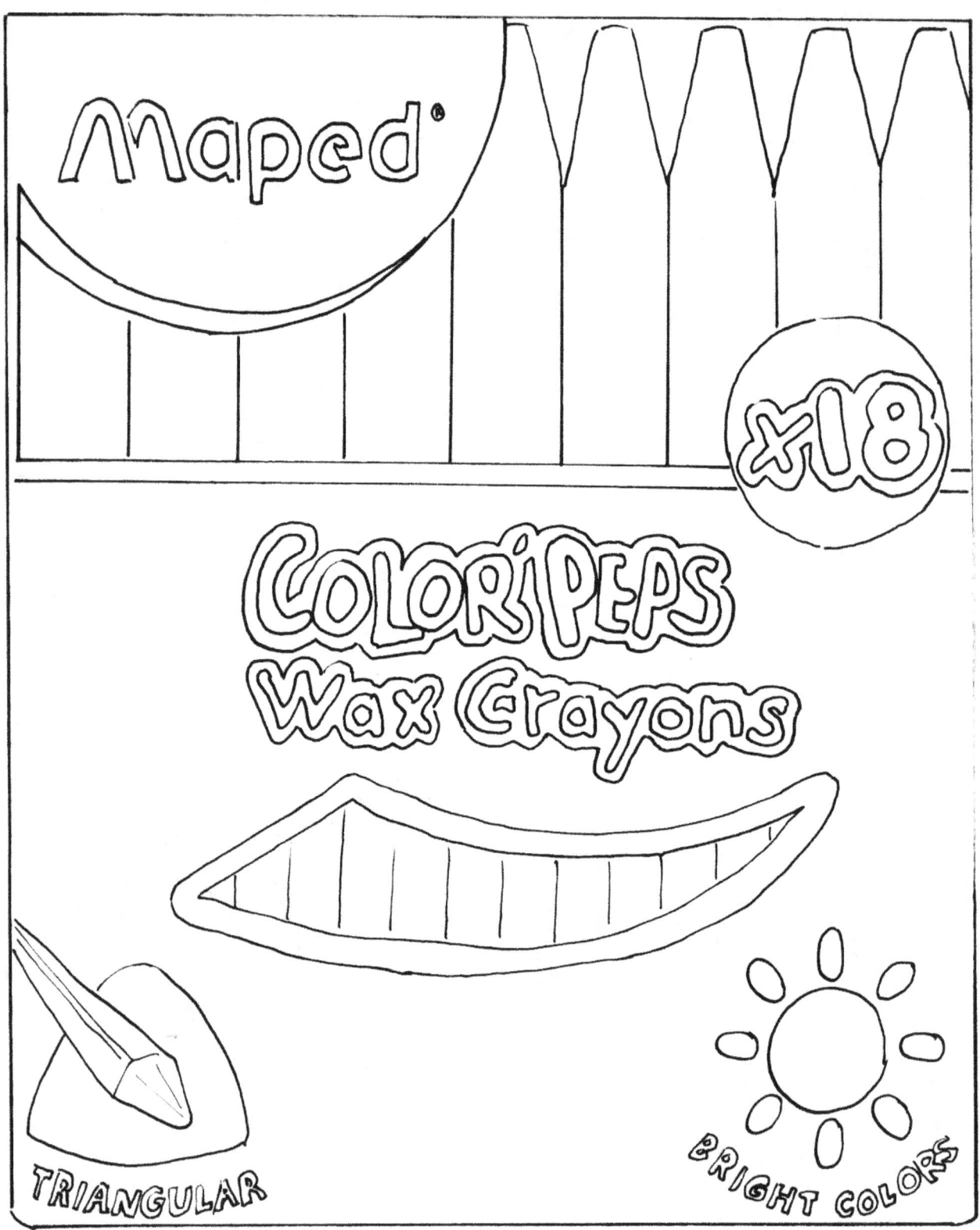

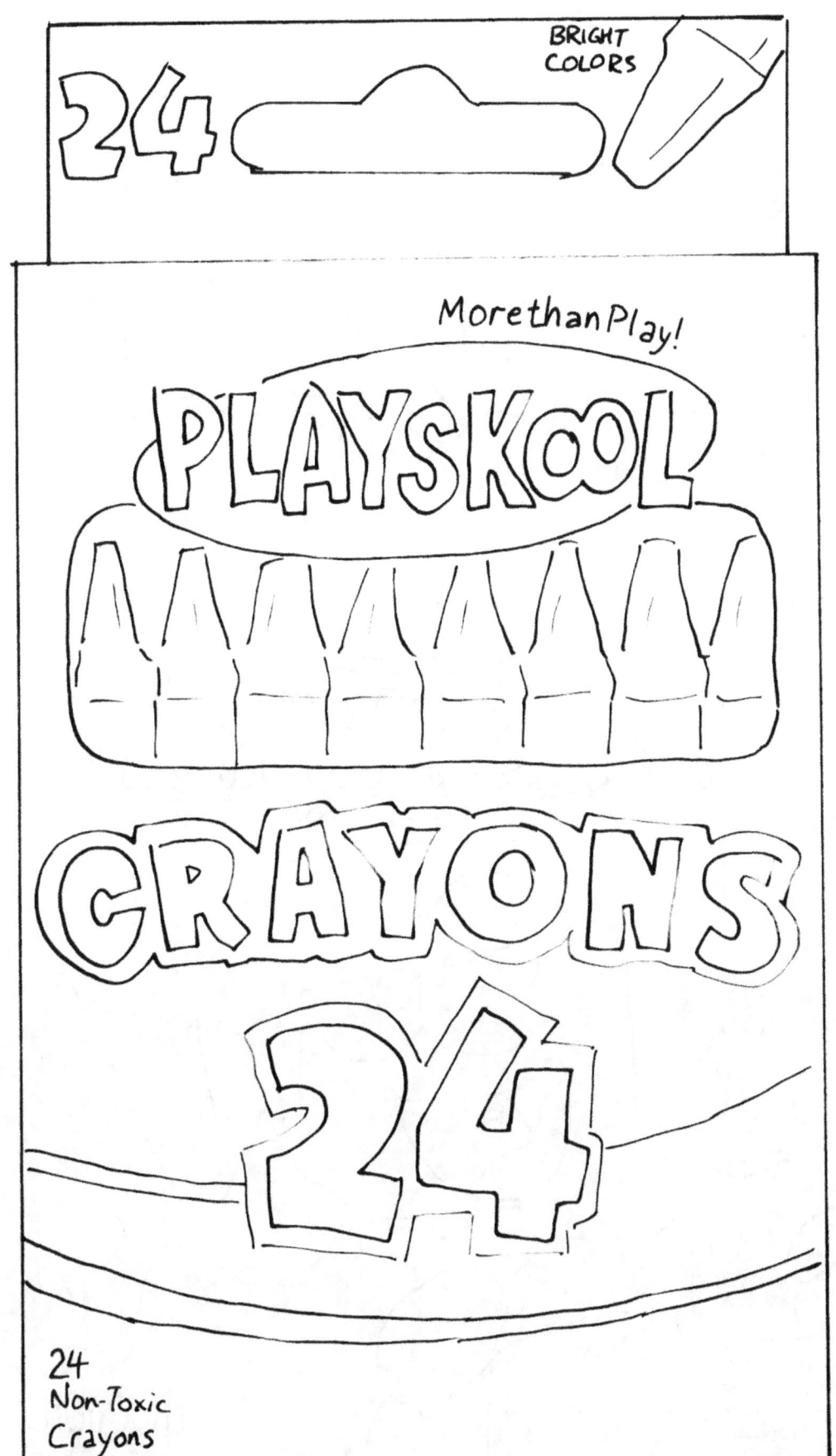

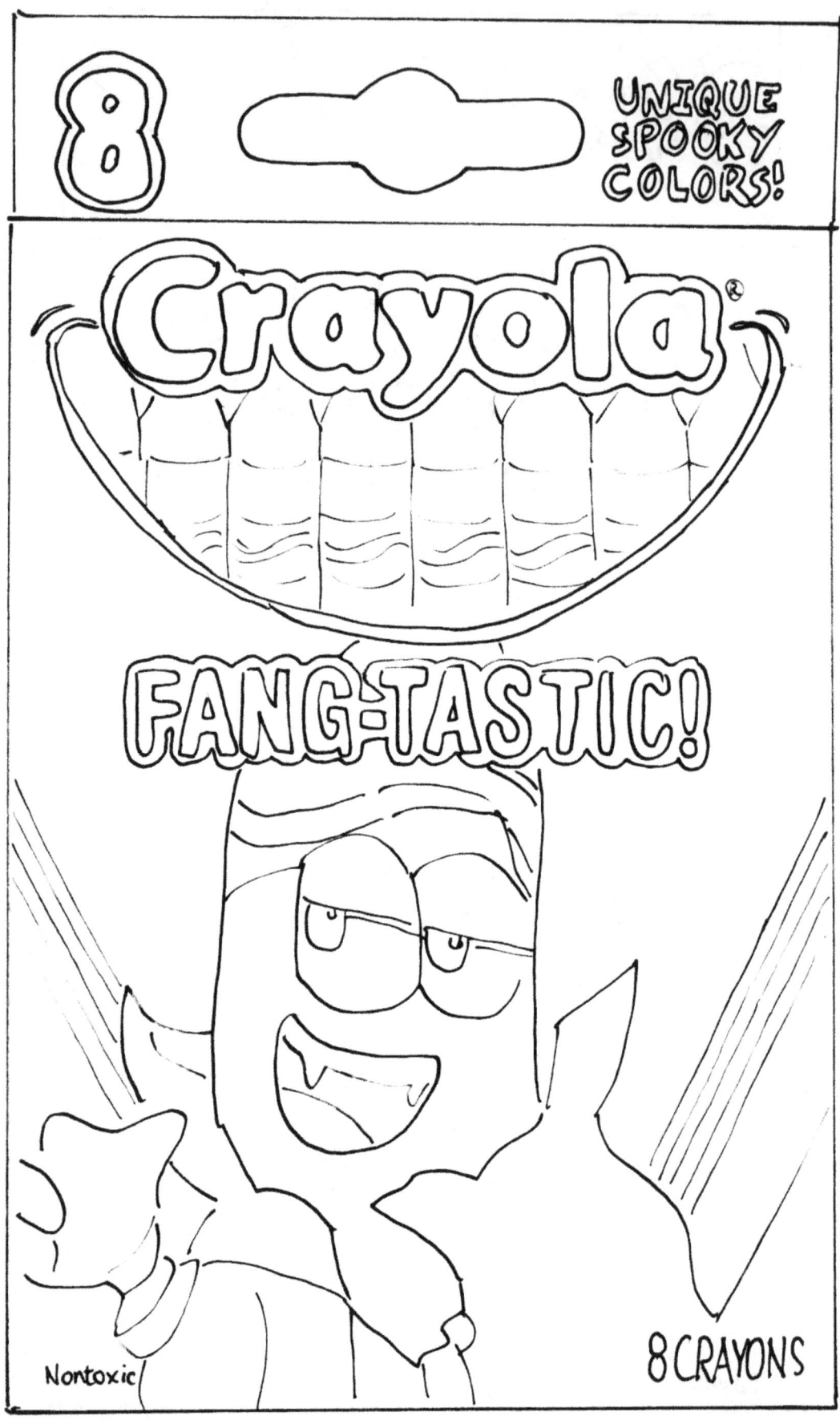

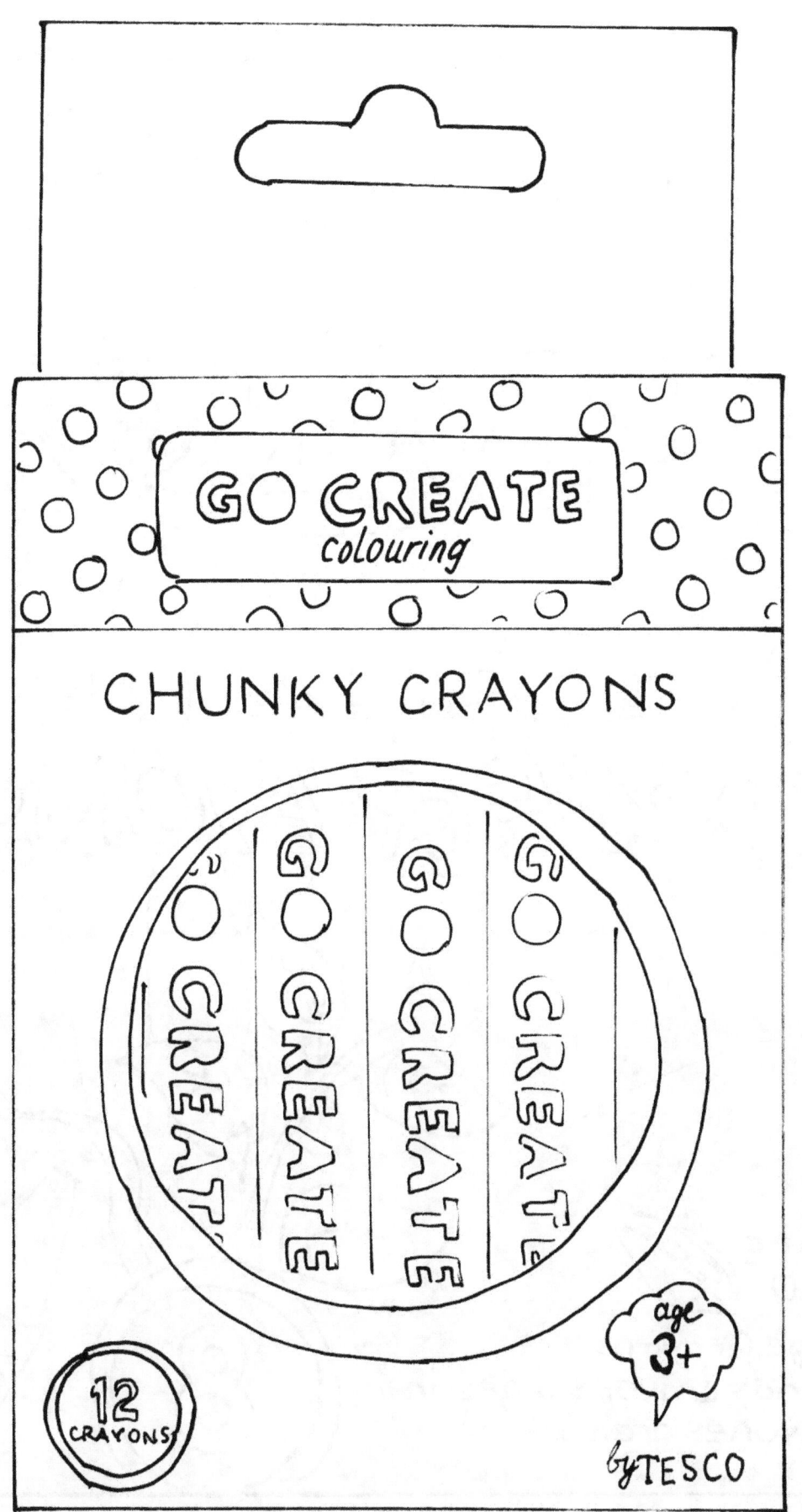

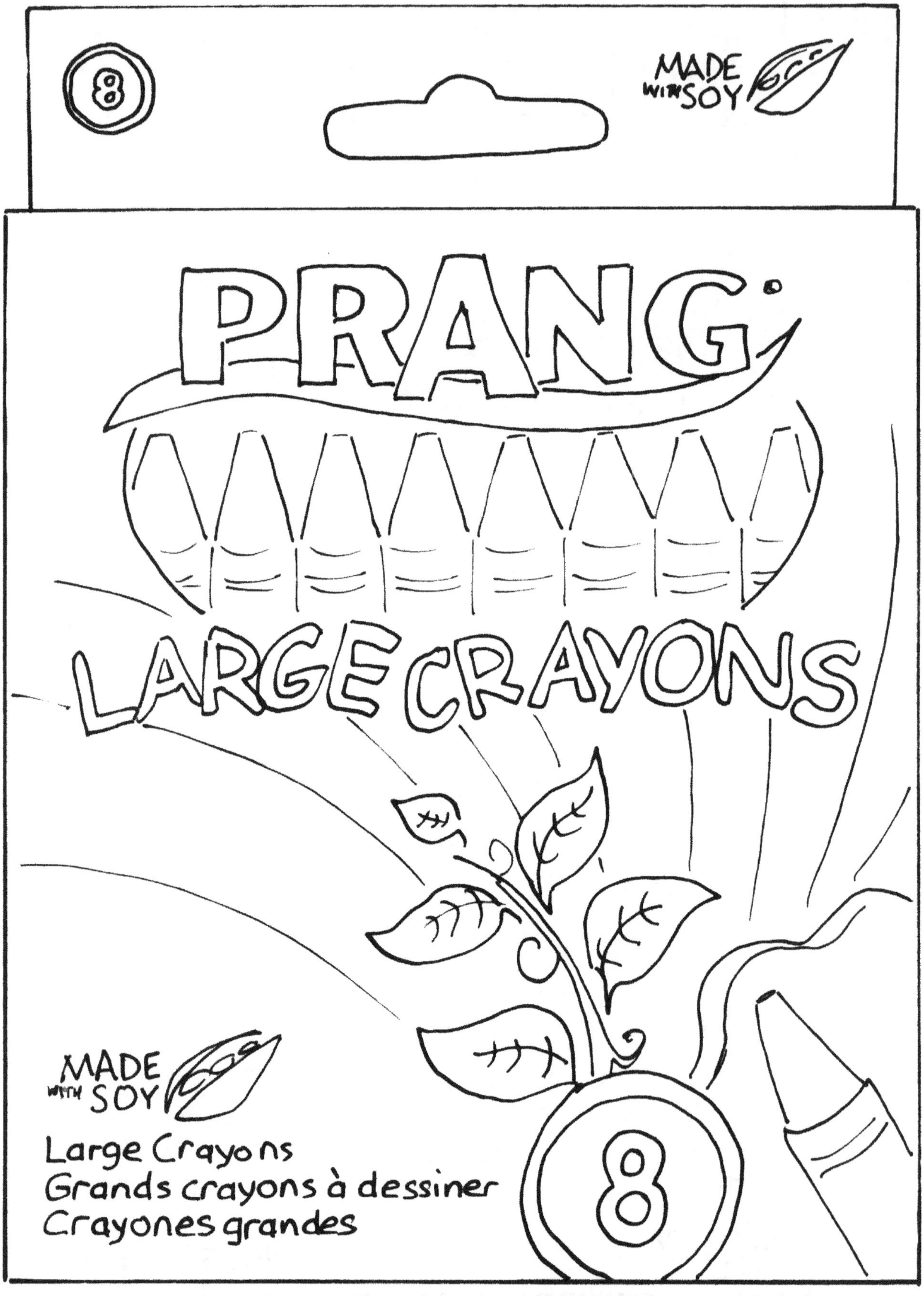

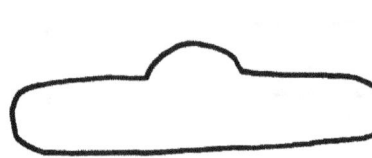

# PRANG

# LARGE CRAYONS

MADE
WITH SOY

Large Crayons
Grands crayons à dessiner
Crayones grandes

8